For Spacious Skies

By Pearl S. Buck

THE GIFTS THEY BRING
  [with Gweneth T. Zarfoss]
THE JOY OF CHILDREN
FRIEND TO FRIEND
  [with Carlos P. Romulo]
MY SEVERAL WORLDS
THE CHILD WHO NEVER GREW
AMERICAN ARGUMENT

TALK ABOUT RUSSIA
WHAT AMERICA MEANS TO ME
OF MEN AND WOMEN
HOW IT HAPPENS
TELL THE PEOPLE
AMERICAN UNITY AND ASIA
FIGHTING ANGEL
THE EXILE

THE CHINESE NOVEL [NOBEL PRIZE LECTURE]

DEATH IN THE CASTLE
THE LIVING REED
FOURTEEN STORIES
COMMAND THE MORNING
LETTER FROM PEKING
COME, MY BELOVED
IMPERIAL WOMAN
THE HIDDEN FLOWER
GOD'S MEN
PAVILION OF WOMEN
KINFOLK
FAR AND NEAR
PEONY

PORTRAIT OF A MARRIAGE
THE PROMISE
DRAGON SEED
TODAY AND FOREVER
OTHER GODS
THE PATRIOT
THIS PROUD HEART
A HOUSE DIVIDED
THE MOTHER
THE FIRST WIFE AND OTHER STORIES
SONS
THE GOOD EARTH
EAST WIND: WEST WIND

VOICES IN THE HOUSE
BRIGHT PROCESSION
THE ANGRY WIFE

THE TOWNSMAN
THE LONG LOVE

ALL MEN ARE BROTHERS [SHUI HU CHÜAN] translated from the Chinese

THE BIG FIGHT
WELCOME CHILD
CHRISTMAS MINIATURE
MY SEVERAL WORLDS
  [Abridged for Younger
  Readers]
THE BEECH TREE
JOHNNY JACK AND HIS BEGINNINGS

ONE BRIGHT DAY
THE BIG WAVE
YU LAN: FLYING BOY OF CHINA
THE DRAGON FISH
THE WATER-BUFFALO CHILDREN
THE CHINESE CHILDREN NEXT DOOR
STORIES FOR LITTLE CHILDREN
THE CHRISTMAS GHOST

FOR SPACIOUS SKIES

SKIES

Journey in Dialogue

PEARL S. BUCK

with

THEODORE F. HARRIS

THE JOHN DAY COMPANY

NEW YORK

Library of Congress Catalogue Card Number: 66–18781

General
11/4/66
10519

Foreword

This book is the record of a journey. It is no ordinary journey. In the first place it was a journey with a purpose. True, it carried me to many places in my own country which I have never seen before. The peculiar circumstances of my multiple life have made me more familiar with the landscapes of Europe and Asia than with those of America. Here, in the land of my ancestry and my birth, my delight in home and family, my absorption in my work, have centered me in a rambling comfortable old house in Pennsylvania.

That I undertook to journey far and wide beyond this beloved spot was because of a return to Asia. Three and a half years ago, to be exact, business took me to Japan to live for many months. Somewhere in those months I accepted an invitation to visit Korea. I was generously treated as always; but on the sidelines of the hospitable busy life of a favored guest, I saw a fringe of sad-faced lonely children, always standing apart. They begged on city streets, they wandered the country roads, ragged and lost, in search of food.

"Who are these?" I asked my hosts.

Their answers were evasive. Alas, I needed no answer. I knew who they were. I recognized them. They were, they are, the children of American servicemen, those young, lonely boys, sent to Asia to fight strange small wars that seem to

7

swell into monstrous combat. In loneliness, in lovelessness, the young Americans search for some slight warmth and comfort before they die in battle. They do not all die, but all live in the presence of death. Somehow among the strangers they find one here, one there, who responds with something else than hatred. Is it any wonder that children are born?

I came back to my own country, my heart full of sorrow and determination. Of piteous children there is a plenty in this world, but among them all these seem to me the most piteous. I do not know a more piteous sight than to see a half-American child wandering the streets of Asia, orphaned because no one wants him, because no one knows what to do with him.

There must be a way, I told myself. That way is described in this book. How was it written? As we traveled the roads, TFH and I, we sat in the back seat of a car driven by a young member of our staff, and we talked this book. That is, we talked and wrote, he the interlocutor. It is a peripatetic book, therefore, a book of written conversation, personal and yet far beyond personalities, for we were and are absorbed in a task far too great for any two persons to accomplish. We send it out as a portrayal and appeal, portrayal of these new children, and appeal for help, in order that they may be saved. They are worth saving, to that I can swear, I who have seen them with my own eyes, and by the thousand. More than half of them die before they are five years old, for only the strong and intelligent can survive the cruel circumstances of their life. But those who survive are superb.

I appeal to you, America!

These are the children of our sons.

Pearl S. Buck

For Spacious Skies

I

TFH: "I've made an appointment for you to give Pearl Buck her first lesson at her home."

That was how it started and from this assignment a whole new world opened. Our entire relationship has been unusual, yours and mine, beginning with that day—unusual, because in all the years during which I had been a teacher of dance I had never been told to go to someone's home to give a lesson. In fact, had such a thing been suggested, I would have refused because of travel time and the fact that only the studio is designed properly with mirrors and floors for good teaching. When I told the manager I would rather not go and asked that he assign another teacher to the task, I had many reasons but I suppose the one most real to me was simply that I had never read *The Good Earth* and had no time to do so. Furthermore, famous persons make me nervous so when I was told I had to teach you I must confess that I faced it as a grim chore.

The wait in your entrance hall gave me no chance for escape either. To have turned and bolted would have brought me face to face with the fact that I'm a devout coward whereas successful teachers with years of experience are supposed to have the poise and confidence that the art of dancing develops. To flee would have meant disgrace and so I decided to face you. You met me with your usual calm and charm, which again confounded me. Students are supposed to be nervous on the first lesson and a teacher must assure the new student that she can learn, that many people take lessons, that this is going to be fun. So, you see, your Oriental calm left me not knowing what to say or do. All I could muster was, "Why do you want to learn to dance?"

PSB: Very well—you say you were terrified of me? I had some terrors, too. In the first place, let me confess what I have never confessed in depth to anyone. By nature I am miserably shy—yes, I am, and don't shake your head when I say so! My mother said that as a small child whenever a stranger came into the room I hid myself in her voluminous skirts with a persistence that embarrassed her. I believe her, for I still have the impulse to flee from a stranger. When you were announced on that hot July day, I wondered why I had ever asked that you come. I was upstairs on the porch, lying in the sun with my head under an umbrella because I always burn red instead of the desired brown.

"Your teacher has come."

That was how the children announced you. I felt the old shy impulse and delayed going downstairs. How had it happened that you, a stranger, were waiting in my house? Then I remembered. It began in India. I had been there for months, working with others on filming R. K. Narayan's brilliant novel, *The Guide*. It had been engrossing work, made lively by the days spent with the cast of three hundred Indians. One day the filming was over and it was time to go home. What would take the place of those months of working and living in so vivid a country? I remember the very day when I asked myself this question. It was a Sunday afternoon, hot and bright. An early monsoon wind, later to bring rain, beat the heavy leaves of coconut palms against my window and piled the surf high in the sea. I lay on my bed, supposedly to rest, but my mind was not resting. What next? How to answer the question? I reflected on what I had not yet done of all I want to do in my life. Among possibilities two personal desires were uppermost that day. I wanted to renew and perfect my French, and yes, I wanted to learn how to dance and to dance well. I like to do things well. I have a passion for excellence. I know no greater satisfaction than to achieve it in whatever I undertake. When I reached home I instructed my secretary to secure the best French teacher available and the best dancing master. She did both. That is how, on a certain summer day, you came to be waiting downstairs.

While I delayed, a further cause for shyness developed. My children raced upstairs to announce in loud consternation that you had red hair.

"Oh, not red hair!" I cried.

Why the consternation? Because, as the children knew, I had an absurd notion about red-haired people, a leftover of my childhood. In China where I grew up, the villain in plays was always a fellow with red hair, typifying the wily Westerner. How many hours as a little girl I had spent sitting on a hard wooden bench beside my Chinese amah, I but one of a great throng who sat watching a play! How fearsome was the red-haired monster on the stage as he shot off guns and punched good Chinese in the jaw! Such experiences had compelled me to develop a dislike for red hair. And was not red an unnatural color for human hair? Living among Chinese, I knew of course that the proper hair color is black. Even my own yellow locks were unfortunate, but red? Impossible!

I felt I really could not go downstairs. Yet, of course, I must and eventually I did. There you stood, young and slim, very polite and resolute, your hair glittering in the sunlight from the open door.

Why do I want to learn to dance? Don't forget I am partly French! Perhaps it's my French grandmother, a petite pretty creature, I am told, dauntless and gay, who left her Huguenot family to marry the young Dutchman who was to be my grandfather. With his parents they came to a Virginia wilderness and the little French wife made the best of it, though very homesick. It was for her that my grandfather came out of the forest wilderness and built the big house in the valley where I was born. Only then, of course, it was in West Virginia, after the line had been drawn dividing Virginia. I never saw my grandmother, for she died before I was born. We have a tintype of her, a wasted small face with enormous dark eyes. But I detect, or imagine, a flicker of the old gaiety.

Why do I want to dance?

When you asked the question, I did not know how to answer. I do something because I want to do it. I like to learn. I enjoy the process of knowing what and how. Dancing is an art as well as exercise. It is lovely to watch, therefore it must be lovely to do. And I felt I could do it. I felt it in my blood and bones, and I wished I had yielded to the impulse long ago. I remember as a young girl, nearly always gay, that after dinner of an evening, or supper, as we called it in our

Southern fashion, I would seize my little sister, seven years younger than I, and dance with her up and down the long wide hall that ran through our house. Singing as I danced, I shaped our steps to the rhythm of the song—no such convenience as records and players in those days—and we danced until we could dance no more. I remember the feeling of relaxation and peace that followed our untutored dancing. There must, then, have been "a spirit in my feet."

I have a memory more grave. When my dearly loved mother was dying, she lay in deep remembering.

"Among the things I wish I had done," she said in her sweet voice, then so faint and faltering, "I wish I had learned to dance. It looks so beautiful. But after that dreadful Civil War in the United States there seemed no time and no reason for dancing."

She had been only twenty-three when in 1880 she married my father and went to China with him. There had been no time or place in that life, either, for dancing.

I remembered her, that hot afternoon in India, and I told myself that I was more fortunate than she, because I do not as yet face death. I have had my sorrows, too, as you now very well know. More than once life has dealt me such blows that I faltered beneath them. I will not speak of personal griefs here, but I will speak of another which, while it is personal, is also universal in certain aspects. It is the unhealed sorrow of the division between my own beloved country, the United States, and my loved other country, China. Anyone who grew up in the era in which my parents and I lived in China knew that some day terrible explosions of independence must burst out in Asia. The two world wars, so weakening to the peoples of the West, undoubtedly hastened the day. Had there not been these wars, empire might have flourished in Asia for another two hundred years, gradually encroaching until the West absorbed the East by the sheer strength of modern power. As it was, Asian peoples saw their opportunity in the exhaustion of the Western peoples, and seizing the period necessary for recovery from the effects of war, they nourished their own determination for freedom and independence and were successful in throwing off Western domination. Into the fury Communism insinuated its own ambitions to make complete the separation, particularly in China where the traditional government had been destroyed by revolution and where Japan had struck for her own Empire, before the Chinese Nationalists could substitute a firm government of their own design. The result is division on a world scale, and division too in my own life, cut off as I am from the years of my childhood and youth. What might have my life been had there been no such division? I suppose I would have lived on both sides of my world, a global commuter. As it is—well, I have learned to live with whatever sorrows come my way, and there is still time in life now for the beauty and joy of dancing.

TFH: It became evident after a short while that you would not bite and that you were not aware of my uneasiness, for which I mentally thanked all my drama teachers. I managed to get through that first visit, resolving meanwhile never again to face you without having a book or at least a story you had written fresh in my mind. A teacher must learn ways to draw a pupil out, in order to adjust to her personality and teach her properly. After all, mine was the only legitimate business where we hold our customers in our arms so the

relationship has to be more personalized than grocery clerking
or shoe fitting. All I managed to learn from you that day,
however, was that the three teen-aged girls hovering about
the library, where we had rolled up the rug to provide floor
space, were your adopted daughters. They seemed highly
amused by the whole procedure. We magic-stepped around
the floor, they tried to conceal their giggles, while I wondered
how these strangely beautiful, not quite Oriental girls came to
be in your farmhouse in the quiet hills of Pennsylvania. I
introduced your first step in rumba. Then I noticed them
trying it on the sidelines and I realized that this was my
perfect opening.

"Your girls seem to have a great deal of ability for dancing,"
I said. "Have you ever thought of giving them lessons?"

What I wanted to ask, was, "How did these girls come to
be your daughters?"

PSB: How did these girls come to be my daughters? I
cannot explain it except that I seem to have a Pied Piper
quality somewhere in my being. I charm children because I
am charmed by them. Far away in my American college days,
I remember declaring to my college mates when we were
dreaming our dreams that I wanted many children, and if I
did not have them myself, I would adopt them. Some of my
afternoons even then were spent in a nearby orphanage, and I
could scarcely tear myself away from the small clinging hands
of lonely children. I spent much time, too, in playing with
and caring for my brother's two children who lived near the
college. My parents were far away in China and I comforted
myself with children. I am fortunate for I have fulfilled my
dreams. My house has been full. The four you saw are the

youngest, and all fathered by American servicemen, the mothers of three of them Japanese women, and the other one German.

How did I get into all this? I suppose because, once I begin, I go deep. I discovered these children of mixed race to be the most needy, the loneliest, and in many ways the loveliest of all children. One by one they came, and now they fill my house with new life.

Yes, my daughters did laugh at me when you gave me my first lesson. Somehow or other they had picked up dancing and were far ahead of me. I must have been very awkward that first day and laughable enough. But, while I am shy, I never mind being laughed at. And my daughters love me while they laugh. They were anxious for me to do well, you know, in spite of laughter. After you were gone they encouraged me by flattery, and I did decide they must have studio lessons, you remember. We would go as a family.

TFH: The lesson ended and I had joined the ranks of your many fans. I simply had to read everything you had ever written. Moreover, I could never be content until I knew the full story of these girls. One of them graciously showed me around the place before I left that evening. The grounds and flowers are beautiful but I was most impressed with how you had converted your barn into a community center for your neighborhood. Complete with kitchen, stage, dance floor and piano, it was there to be used. My old terror came back, however, when I looked at the bookshelves that lined the walls of the barn and realized that nearly all of the thousands of books were indeed Pearl S. Buck books, translated into many languages, most of which I had never heard of. I

18

remember I asked you how many books you had written and how you did it.

PSB: I apologize for all those books by explaining that they are translations. As you know, authors are always given a certain number of copies of their books. When the books are translated into many languages—and I fear I am the most translated living American author in the literary field—the house fills up with books. In desperation we built shelves in the barn. As for your question, how many books have I written, how does one answer such questions? To say that a writer is born, not made, is a truism. Yet I was never a scribbler. Even as a child, I did not write for writing's sake. I wrote because there was something I wanted to tell—a story, an idea, a feeling. As a young girl I wrote poetry more often than prose. I remember the joy of discovering that sometimes my poetry was good, that it was real. I remember the exact day, even the hour, of the discovery. I was thirteen years old, that age so delicately and precariously poised between child and girl. My parents, thinking I had not enough companionship with children of my own age, especially non-Chinese, had put me for a few months into a small private school in Kuling, a mountain resort established by Westerners in order to escape the heat of the Yangtse delta. I suppose I learned something there, but I do not remember that I did. What I remember is that, in that templed landscape, without my family and surrounded by strangers, suddenly I found myself. I began to write poetry, not childhood verse.

I hoped and doubted. Was my poetry good or did I imagine it was? In need of confirmation, I went to a teacher whom I trusted and put into her hands a few short poems. I still see her clearly. She was young and sensitive, tall, slender, auburn-haired. She took the poems to her room and I waited for two interminable days. On the second evening she beckoned me to the veranda—a lovely evening, I remember, the mountains violet against the sunset sky—and she gave me back my poems and left me. Attached to them was a short note. I read it, my heart beating. It was not the criticism I had feared.

"Keep writing, little poet," she told me.

I ran to my room to be alone. I read the poems over and over again and with them the precious note. Then, my heart full, I wrote a letter to my mother.

"Dear Mother," I wrote, and I can remember every word of that letter—I have that kind of memory, "Miss Katharine says I am a poet. 'Keep writing,' she says. Now I know what I am meant to be."

When my mother's letter came in answer, she was calm and I felt too practical. "It is nice that you are a poet," she wrote me, "but remember your father and I want a good report card."

I was not exactly hurt, but I went underground, so to speak. I never told anyone again that I was a poet. I merely continued to write. That is what I have done ever since. How many books? Does it matter? I think not. Each is written out of an experience, an hour, a moment, when life struck me hard and deep, and I put it into a book as truly as I could.

Yes, I know the best authors are not supposed to write many books. They are supposed to bring out one gem every five years or so—better every ten! Some even labor for twenty and produce one book. But what if one has more than that to say and more to tell? Suppose life is overwhelmingly rich and one delights to portray it to the best of one's ability in all its manifold variety? Well, one is called prolific; a term of reproach, it seems, for a writer. And one keeps on writing.

TFH: After that first lesson I remember booking the second and beginning the frantic search for knowledge of the evidently great but distressingly mysterious woman I had met. I have made it a practice all my life that when I want to learn something I find the person who should know and ask questions. Ha! It has always worked before, but not with you. Everyone I asked, bar none, began the answer with, "Well, she wrote *The Good Earth*."

Most of my information came from one of my students who had been in the English Department at Princeton some years ago. She at least told me you had written many best sellers, although how many she did not know. She also told me that Welcome House was some sort of agency for children. From others I gathered such choice bits of misinformation as "she has had three husbands, the first of whom was Frank Buck." Or "she has two retarded children," or "she has an enormous family of fourteen," and "she married some Chinese man."

PSB: But this is shocking! I had no idea that such strange misinformation floats about in the lower air. Poor Frank Buck! I never met him, and he is dead, but some people still believe that all who bear that name must belong to him. Only the other day in a hotel lobby a woman came up to me and said:

"I work here and this is my day off but I heard you were here and I just had to see you. I've so enjoyed your books but weren't you afraid of all those wild animals your husband brought back from jungles?"

In case anyone wants to know how I came by a strange name, and one not my own, the story is told in my book, *My Several Worlds*. As for the rest of it, I do have three sons, all very much alive, and I do have a big family, thank God, one child by birth and nine adopted. I have been twice married, both times to white Americans, et cetera, et cetera.

But tell me, why didn't you come to the source of information? Why didn't you ask me?

TFH: Ask you? Around you I was still so nervous I could scarcely think of my own name, let alone the questions I wanted to ask. Finally, although this information, or misinformation, came from fairly intelligent people, I knew I had to read for myself. Someone did tell me that your autobiography was entitled *My Several Worlds* and I decided to read it first. Those who are familiar with teachers of dance know that the hours are long, and shopping becomes a major problem. So I took to the telephone to locate the book. Try though I did, I could not find *My Several Worlds* or, in fact, any other Pearl S. Buck hardback book. I remember wondering how a book could get to be a best seller if no one could buy it. One clerk in a store in downtown Philadelphia finally told me she had several paperbacks and one of them was the one I sought. Then getting it was a problem, for I was ten miles away. The shop was open late that night, however, so all I could do was to drive in after ten o'clock when the studio closed. I bought seven paperbacks. One was *Fourteen Stories*. I couldn't wait any longer. I went into a restaurant and drank coffee until I had finished the first story, "A Certain Star." I remember the beauty of the story and I wondered how it came to be written.

PSB: It is an old complaint of authors and their readers against book sellers that books cannot be found when wanted. The charge is just, I believe, at least to an author. All too quickly our books go out of print and are not reprinted. And paperbacks do not take the place of the more permanent hardbacks, especially when a reader wants to build a lasting library. Publishers retaliate with two retorts; first, they maintain that even though a book is in stock, awaiting orders, bookstore clerks are too lazy to take the trouble to send in an order and it is easier merely to persuade a customer to buy some other book. Second, the publisher maintains that he cannot afford to keep a book in print after sales drop to a certain level. The result of such excuses—and they are excuses, to a certain degree—is that an author may find his, or her, lifework reduced to a handful of paperbacks, as ephemeral as yesterday's snowflakes. This is a situation which the author should protest with vigor. Speaking generally, it is destructive to our culture that books are not kept alive in permanent bindings. Paperbacks are excellent in their place, but hardbacks should always be available. Fortunately for me, my publisher is an exception. My books are in hardback and in libraries all over the country.

As for my long short story, "A Certain Star," it was written out of that period of my life when I was following closely the development of nuclear fission through the atomic bomb. This phase was enlightened by my friendship with the distinguished scientist, Arthur Compton, to whom I owe my first nuclear education. Out of the years of our friendship— he is now dead, alas—I wrote also my novel, *Command the Morning*. I sent him the manuscript of that novel before publication, asking for his suggestions and criticisms. He read it carefully and wrote me a note which I keep among my treasures as a source of pride. Here it is:

"This is a good job. I'm naturally pleased that you find in me a suitable 'hero' around whom to build your story. But I'd rather not comment about what you say about the hero. After all, this is your story!

"Except for a few minor factual corrections, the only significant change I have suggested is on the last page, where I altered the words quoted from me to make them more in character. All good wishes. AHC"

Later it came about that a national weekly magazine asked me for a Christmas story. Christmas in my big household is always a heartwarming occasion, and I am frankly sentimental about it. I said I would write the story, and it grew out of my interest in nuclear scientists as human beings. The magazine gave its entire issue to the story, and afterwards reprinted it in a small book. I take a modest pride in any bit of success, and I am glad this was your first among my stories. There is a considerable amount of me in that story, scattered about in several persons but all portraying the manifold aspects of one inquiring mind. This is the way of a writer, for how else can one bear the pressures of endless wonder and curiosity, the capacity for conflicting emotions and feelings, the wayward impulses, which make up a born writer's personality?

TFH: Well, "A Certain Star" did it for me. I was hooked! That same night after I went to bed I started *My Several Worlds*. Even with a lesson booked at 10 A.M., an early hour for one who works until ten and eleven each night, I simply could not stop. My lifelong friend, Jimmy, then my housemate, started *Imperial Woman* at the same time. I remember while I read that I was aware of the thin strip of light beneath his door. I knew that he, too, couldn't stop. When I went to sleep finally at six in the morning I remember vaguely wondering how he would manage to rise at seven to go to his job. When I rose at half past eight, I went to his room and found him sound asleep, his light on, his alarm blaring, *Imperial Woman* resting on his chest.

I learned many facts that night. I learned that the house in which I met you is Green Hills Farm. You don't have a sign on your mailbox, you know! I learned that you had traveled a great deal, that you had lived many years in China, although you were not born there, and that you had married your publisher. I remember thinking at the same time how very clever that was of you!

PSB: Clever? We both knew it was the worst possible thing for an author and publisher to do. He was furious with himself and grumbled about it.

"I'd never believe I could be such a fool as to fall in love with my best-selling author—but damn it, that's what I've done!"

I repudiated all responsibility. "Don't blame me," I told him. "It's the last thing I want, too."

We were married for twenty-five happy years and we only laughed when one of our sons, aged fourteen, reported the following conversation with his best friend of the same age.

FRIEND: What does your father do?
SON: He's a publisher.
FRIEND: What does your mother do?
SON: She's a writer.
FRIEND: What a racket!

The miracle was that each of us maintained an entirely separate existence in the midst of a gay family life. At proper times he was only my publisher and I was only an author. He had a critical rather than creative mind and once went so far as to decide not to publish one of my novels that was already in galleys, because he felt it was perhaps too personal. I heroically agreed to its suppression then, but now, after these many years, it is soon to be published.

TFH: Still, I could not find all the little answers I wanted to know, such as what you like and what are your dislikes, which is your favorite language, what language you think in, what Welcome House is and why. A million and one whys and whats I knew I must find out or suffer the fate of the proverbial cat.

I drove out for my second appointment with you and my head was whirling as I was storing up all of these questions to fire at you the moment I saw you. The nearer I got, however, the more nervous I became so that finally as you appeared in your entrance hall that other proverbial cat did his work on my tongue. All I could blurt out was, "Good evening, Miss Buck, will you tell me something about Friendship House?" Instantly I was horrified and I felt my heart skip as I realized my error but you graciously corrected me and with great patience began to tell me about "Welcome House." Many times since I've known you I've thought to myself, "Patience, thy name is Pearl."

PSB: You know so well, now, what Welcome House is that it would be strange to talk about it again. Briefly, it is an adoption agency that I founded many years ago, with the help of friends, especially for orphans of mixed American-Asian ancestry, in order that they might have good and loving families. This purpose, still primary, has been broadened to include physically handicapped children, older children and so-called unadoptable children. It is amazing and heartening to discover that families can always be found, if one is patient in the search.

You may ask, as I am often asked, why a writer concerns herself with such activities. I have asked myself the same question and upon examining my own reasons, I have come to the conclusion that they are artistic rather than humanitarian. I have an artist's love of order—order in the cosmic sense. It is disorderly to have children without families, disorderly to permit human beings to be lost. Disorder is destructive, the very composition is unhappy. Perhaps composition is the accurate word rather than order. Children with nowhere to go, no one to belong to, break the composition of human life. It seems necessary for me to try to restore order and therefore composition, whether it be of a room or a life. This is happiness.

TFH: I remember your lesson went quite well that evening but I vowed I would, somehow, persuade you to come into the studio. I thought that if I could get you into my own bailiwick I could somehow cope better with my cowardice. The beautiful things in your house made me feel strange—almost as if they were sacred. I felt it was wrong somehow to walk on your lovely rugs, brought from your home in China. I remember asking if those were in fact the ones you wrote about in *My Several Worlds* and how they came to be where they are.

PSB: Yes, I did tell about those rugs in that book, but what I did not tell was how nearly I lost them. They reached New York safely, were inspected at customs in the presence of my secretary and then sent by express to my rambling old farmhouse eighty miles away. When they arrived, five bales were missing! I knew exactly which ones were missing, for they had all been in my Chinese home. I reported the loss to the local express office and with considerable indignation.

"Those rugs came across two hundred miles of war-torn China, across the Pacific Ocean, through the Panama Canal to New York. Now, within the last eighty miles they are lost," I said over the telephone.

"Madame," the reply was, "kindly send us a bill and we will send our check."

"A check can't pay for those rugs," I retorted. "They were made in Peking."

"Madame, if you will send us a bill—"

"I will not! I want my rugs."

This conversation was repeated again and again during several weeks. A different voice always insisted that I send a bill. I always refused. Then one day I decided to report the whole matter to the president of the express company himself. I did not know him, but secretaries yielded, one by one. I heard his voice over the wires and I told my story.

"You are quite right," he said. "You must have your rugs, and I will see that you get them. But it will take a little time. Be patient."

I was patient for several months during which he called now and again to say he was working. At last, one unexpected day, the rugs arrived intact. What did I learn from the experience? That I must always go to the top when I want to accomplish something! How reassuring it is to hear that voice at the top, promising me that what I want done will be done—bless all men at the top!

TFH: You did agree to come into the studio for future

lessons but said you would feel better if you had a few lessons alone first. I felt better myself then, for I knew I would get my wish and that I would eventually not be trying to teach you in surroundings that made me feel more nervous and strange than I might have otherwise felt. You have a great deal of ability as a student. I remember how amusing I thought it was when I realized that one of the statements to instill confidence suggested for use by teachers applied to you quite truthfully. That statement is, and I've heard it a million times, "You know, you really are a very good dancer. You just don't know what to do with your feet!" That's a marvelous statement, for it never fails to prompt a smile. It is true, in fact, for dancing is really quite simple to learn, after a pupil perceives that it is more than a series of disconnected gyrations. But the pupil must have as much confidence in his own ability to learn as in his teacher's ability to teach. I remember trying to account for your unusual ability, and noticing the beautiful piano in your library I asked if you played and had had much instruction in music.

PSB: Music is a deep creative force in my life. I inherit it, I suppose, through my mother. She came of a gifted musical family and she herself had a lovely clear soprano voice. When she was married and went to China, her eldest brother, my Uncle Cornelius, gave her a Mason and Hamlin organ for a wedding present. It was shipped to her home in China, and there I learned my notes and how to play. Somehow, by the time I was six, she contrived to buy a piano. It was English, I remember, a Moutrie, and I transferred myself, at least partly, from organ to piano. She was my piano teacher and through her I learned to know the great classical composers. Beethoven and Chopin are still my favorites.

In a sense, I live my life to music. When I am weary, I go to the piano. In the evenings, when my daughters are busy with schoolwork upstairs in their rooms, my house seems too big now and very silent. Then I turn to the piano and play. In justice to myself, I also practice, for I try each week to take a lesson from my German music master. He is delightful and he is strict. Of course he thinks I should devote myself to my piano. Two hours a day is all I can manage and lucky if I do that, but he dreams of five hours or even six. I am dissatisfied, too, but I know it is foolish for me to dream. Life has put demands upon me and I cannot indulge myself in a favorite avocation.

To remember again, my mother when I was an impatient girl of fifteen or so, persuaded me to buy a guitar at a music shop in Shanghai. She bought one also for my adopted Chinese sister and she taught us both to play. She had some sort of romantic fondness for the guitar, I suspect, a leftover, perhaps from some early lover whom she could not quite forget. Because I wanted to please her, I learned how to play the guitar and to sing Western folk songs and ballads with it, but I never really enjoyed it. Rather than the guitar as a stringed instrument, I enjoyed my Chinese harp, which a Chinese teacher taught me how to play. It lay flat upon floor or table and the strings were not plucked but were struck lightly with two slender sticks of bamboo, giving forth a sweet high sound. I learned Chinese songs, too, and enjoyed their vigor. But I am really a pianist and among my honorary degrees I value much the one from the Coombs College of Music in Philadelphia. Though I don't deserve it, I like to have it, nevertheless.

Yes, music is my chief pleasure.

TFH: I found you very easy to talk to, much to my surprise. I began to discover that your mind works like a busy little animal but with the capacity of a sponge. It races around, rooting out each available bit of knowledge on a most astounding array of subjects, then quietly soaks it up and waits to be squeezed. I've seen you, after weeks or even months have passed, drop some choice "Pearl of wisdom" (no pun intended, but I'm sure that phrase originated with someone trying to describe you), that I've heard you pick up from this person or that on one of your frequent brain-picking jaunts. I even commented once on how inquisitive you are and it brought out of you a perfectly charming story of a childhood clockwatching stint. Everything in life has a way of compensating for something else, according to Emerson, and I suppose your compensation is that in exchange for your very inquisitive nature you seem perfectly willing to answer any and all questions. I began to lose my fear. On the third visit to your home I commented on the strange Chinese desk in your library, with its latticework and stiff, uncomfortable-looking chair. I asked if there was something special about it.

PSB: You have put a good deal of my life into those few lines. Yes, I am an inquisitive creature, I want to know and to understand. My tool is the question. I cannot restrain myself from asking questions—I never could. I remember that my poor mother, always patient, grew quite frantic with me sometimes in my childhood.

"For fifteen minutes," she would declare, "you may not ask one question. I need a rest."

I must have been very small, for I remember I always drew my little wicker chair close to the big clock on the wall and folding my hands I watched intently while the minutes ticked away. Promptly on the quarter hour I was ready.

"Mother, why—"

And so forth. To this day, as I very well know, I am insatiable for knowledge. You are patience itself when I ask questions of you about your own most unusual life. I am half-ashamed of myself but not quite. It is so good to know. I come away from a day spent in a nuclear physics installation, for example, refreshed by new knowledge. I haunt space centers and plague the young scientists there with my questions. Why should I care to know every detail about a space vehicle? I shall never travel in one. Yet I must know. My memory, fortunately excellent, is crammed with useless knowledge. And you have often laughed at me because a few minutes with any stranger is long enough for me to discover his history, and his dreams to boot. Yet it may not be entirely useless, for though I collect such information as instinctively as a squirrel collects nuts, it serves me. Again and again when I am in ferocious creativity, voices, looks, ways, landscapes, rise to the surface of my subconscious mind and are of use in making a character visible in a novel.

As for that desk, I found it half a lifetime ago in a furniture shop in an ancient winding street of the old city of Nanking. I knew the moment I saw it that I must have it. It is of heavy black wood, and it is finished with Ningpo varnish, a matchless varnish only to be had in China. You see the Chinese windsor chair that goes with it? I bought that, too. The shopkeeper told me that both pieces had belonged to a famous and aged scholar, the latticework to keep his feet away from cold tiled floors. My study in those days, always private, was on the third floor of my house in China and there the desk and chair were moved. I had the desk set to face a wide gable window, from whence I could see the sweep of the city within its own great wall, and beyond that the purple flanks of the mountains. There in that quiet place at that desk I wrote four books in this order: *The Exile, East Wind: West Wind, The Good Earth, The Mother.*

I never thought in those years that some day the desk and chair would stand here, in this American house, so far away.

TFH: By the end of your third lesson you were dancing box and magic steps with the greatest ease. You had mastered rumba and tango and even the elusive rhythm of the cha-cha. I'll never forget how funny it struck me when I commented on the strange expression on your face as you went through the required cha-cha maneuvers and you said:

"I'm just never able quite to make up my mind that the time has come when I must cha-cha."

At any rate, I was able to convince you, I think, for I'm never altogether sure who does the convincing with us, that your confidence had improved to the point that the time had come for you to visit the studio. You agreed, and the appointment was set. Time passed slowly for me before the day arrived, for now I must admit I had been quite won over by you and your girls and had developed great pride, and perhaps had achieved a sort of status, in the fact that I was your teacher. I was most anxious for you to come to the studio so that I could show off all we had accomplished in so short a time. I must also confess, however, that I found myself even more nervous and apprehensive than before for fear you wouldn't like our studio and might not come back.

In you came at last, flanked by your four girls, and looking very regal. You headed straight for one of the benches that lined the walls of our main ballroom and attached yourself to it as though it were the Imperial Throne of China. Looking neither to the right nor left, you sat and waited the two or three minutes before your lesson was to begin. The studio had been all hustle-bustle and excitement that day, waiting for your arrival, and I've often wondered how you felt on that first visit.

The bench eventually became known as Pearl Buck's Bench and no one would sit there when the time drew near for your lesson, for you always went straight to it as though it were some haven in a storm.

PSB: I made for that bench, of course, because I was shy when I came into the studio. I wonder if this incurable shyness comes from the circumstances of my life? Without at all wanting it, I have always been compelled to be someone not like those around me. In the first place, I was the child of parents who were notable in their native region in West Virginia. Added to this was the fact that they chose to be missionaries and to China, of all places. There never had been missionaries in either of their ancestral families and why should there be, when life was comfortable in big houses set in wide lands? Beyond this, I was a child especially welcome in the family because three little children had died the sudden death of the tropical climate before I was born. A child always knows when she is especially welcome. She breathes it in the atmosphere. Again beyond this, I was an American child in a Chinese community, a white child among a brown people. Wherever I went, I was looked at, commented upon and made conspicuous. This was not done unkindly, but with simple interest, followed by friendly affection. In American college days of course I was different from my college mates. I came from another world than theirs. They flocked to look at me, to inquire of my strangeness, and again, not unkindly, I was set apart.

I was set apart, too, by something in myself, which I cannot define. Schoolwork was so easy for me that I felt my classmates envious and this embarrassed me. I took prizes without trying and was pained to discover that there were persons who did not like me the better for such success. I remember that I took the senior prizes for both prose and poetry at my college graduation. No one had ever done this before, and since these were much-coveted prizes there was criticism to the effect that they should not in any event have been given to one person. I felt somehow that the fault was mine. Years later the same sort of criticism fell upon me when the Nobel Prize for literature was given me and I felt almost apologetic for having received it—foolish, but it was part of the old sense of being made different from those around me.

Among my children my fourth daughter had been the one most sensitive to the difference which sets me apart without any wish of my own. She said one day, after autograph seekers pressed me on a street:

"One thing I know—I'll never let myself be famous."

"It is not a question of letting," I told her. "It comes, whether one wants it or not."

For me the importance lies in being able to do one's work, which in my case is writing books. Yet I am now so accustomed to whatever it is that sets me apart that I walk in an atmosphere of my own, detaching myself from others—too much so, perhaps, for I like people and often long to be close to someone. I realize this cannot be.

When I returned to my own country to live, the situation was hopeless. I was already what is called "famous," and therefore marked wherever I went. I do not know how others meet this situation, but I developed a habit of going quietly and directly to my destination and my business, with the subconscious hope that I could avoid conversation of an exclamatory nature. This, in general, is why I went straight to the bench that day and sat there, looking neither to left nor right, and thinking my own thoughts until you came, with your usual welcoming smile, to begin the lesson. Of course I did not know the bench was "my" bench.

TFH: Another of the tasks a teacher must accomplish in dancing is to stop a student from thinking out each step. While learning the figure she must in fact be able to picture it mentally in order to dance it. After this, she must learn not to concentrate. The reason is rather obvious. Dancing is a social art in this country and a certain amount of conversation is necessary. But counting quick-quicks, or one-two-three-fours is not a proper reply for one to make while the usual niceties are being said by the teacher. So the student, who often feels that from the waist down she has nothing but several left feet, must also learn to talk while dancing. This process is like patting one's head and rubbing one's tummy or vice versa and I am sure that students often wish that their teachers would just be quiet and stop asking multitudes of questions that must be answered unless one is willing to be rude. A teacher's success is dependent therefore to a large extent on his conversational ability. We learn early that one of the quickest ways to get persons to talk is to ask questions about themselves.

With you, of course, this made my job most pleasant. There were many questions still that I had stored up and I was very anxious to have them answered. To my surprise and delight, I found you willing to talk and as I overcame my fear of you I began what I hoped would not seem like a third-degree session. I was so fascinated by your vast and different

36

life experiences that I could hardly contain myself from one lesson to the next. There were many small, seemingly unimportant, things I wanted to know. For example, in your books I noticed a difference in sentence structure between your Chinese stories and the American novels you published under the name of John Sedges. This difference puzzled me until that day of your first visit when, while trying to divert your attention away from your toes, I asked how many languages you spoke. That led to the question I really wanted answered which was:

"Well, speaking several languages, tell me what language do you think in?"

PSB: Of course if I had known or even suspected that your questions were part of your teaching technique I would not have answered so willingly or easily. I suppose I was surprised by your natural friendliness, as I had seen it exhibited toward everyone about you, and I responded to it as well as I could. There is not much opportunity in my life for personal conversation. Perhaps it would not have been so easy with you if we had not been moving together in the relaxing rhythms of dancing. But the truth is, I have observed that you are able to interest yourself in anyone in your vicinity. I am sure that having to teach many different kinds of women, young and old, has developed this versatility. It is an asset and I have tried to learn how to have it—not too successfully, I fear, for I have my decided preferences in people and cannot conceal them too gracefully!

As for thinking in languages, I think in several. When I am writing a novel in a Chinese setting and with Chinese characters I think in Chinese, which is in a sense my native tongue, since I first learned to speak in that language. This may account for the difference in sentence structure which you notice. When I write in the American or Western scene, my characters not Chinese, I think in English. The sentence structure is very different. For example, English has many more prepositions than Chinese has, and I have never quite grown used to such a plethora of prepositions, each so exact in its use.

It is not unusual, this thinking in different languages. I do it to some extent in German, and always in French, when I am with French people. There is a wonderful moment when one is learning a new language. It is the moment when one no longer translates to one's self, but thinks directly in the new language. This is to enter into a new world, a new comprehension. It is one of life's exciting moments.

TFH: Ha! You accuse me of being inquisitive and interesting myself in anyone and everything? Never in a lifetime would I have the courage to ask the questions of people that you do. I don't know whether you realize it but about ninety percent of your conversation begins with Why? Where? What? Which? When? Who? How? After the first five minutes with a person, you are apt to know everything about him. Of course I must also admit that many times when we attend public functions together I've noticed that people give you very personal and totally unsolicited facts about themselves and their lives. I remember, for example, the meaning-to-be-entertaining lady at a dinner one night who began, quite without provocation, to describe to you the intricate details of her husband's ulcer and of the ordeal of living with a man who has one. At each polite nod of your head she came out with some new description of his agony. With great enthusiasm she told of his nervous stomach and how she

38

would try to entice him to eat, etc., etc., etc. Poor fellow! We agreed that he seemed a rather calm forty pounds overweight. I know your dinner was almost unbearable with this steady barrage. On the other hand, I've left you engaged in idle conversation with a friendly stranger while I went to get you some refreshments and returned no more than three minutes later to have you ready to tell me where he was born, what kind of work he does, how many children he has, what he is doing, where he is, how he came to be there, etc., etc., etc. I suppose it must be true, as you have said, that the whole world is searching for a sympathetic ear.

PSB: I assure you that I am not consciously collecting material for books, if that is what you mean to insinuate! And I have no concern with gossip. It is true that I am deeply interested in human beings. Most of them have a problem of some sort in their lives, and therefore a secret longing which they will discuss with a stranger. True, all they tell me is stored away in the depths of my insatiable maw of mind and memory, perhaps never to be used, perhaps to be used in fragmentary form. The shaping of a book is a long process. It begins like the shaping of a star in space, a nebula of whirling particles which by their centrifugal movement achieve a form. This gradually focuses toward a solid shape and there is entity.

In somewhat the same way ideas accumulate in a writer's brain. They cluster about a character, in my case, and through him the story develops. Slowly the fragments begin to form a solid whole. This solid whole is a book. These ideas, these books, develop through a period of years. The writing is only the final act.

TFH: By this time I was completely wrapped up in your

every lesson. My friends must have found me quite different. My every conversation began with "Miss Buck says," "Miss Buck does," "Miss Buck this," "Miss Buck that." I feared for awhile that they might grow tired of my enthusiastic chatter but they were evidently as interested as I, for their first remarks were more often than not, "What does Miss Buck do, say or think about thus and such or the other?"

Time passed with me reading your books and planning all the questions I wanted to ask about them. I felt so wonderful when I was with you—still do, as a matter of fact! It was like standing on the edge of a great forest wanting to know everything in its depths, yet knowing that if you did go in you might get lost and never return to this everyday, workaday world. One hesitates to step into the forest when one knows he may not want to leave. Indeed this has happened. Many times since then I've said I must rewrite the "Cinderella" story and call the leading character "Cinder Fella." I remember that the first book that ever left me with tears of joy at the end was *The Townsman*. It is such a perfect book. Tears have come many times since with your books but I've never been able to get over the feeling of great loss I had after *The Townsman*. I miss Jonathan as though he had indeed been my dearest friend. I must discover how he came to be.

PSB: The foreword to *American Triptych* explains how Jonathan came to be. Here it is entire:

Some years ago I woke one morning to find myself strangely oppressed. I felt suddenly that I was no longer a free individual. I had been cast in a mold. I had written so many books about Chinese people that I had become known as a writer only about China. This was natural enough and nobody's fault. When I began to write I knew no people intimately except the Chinese. My entire life had been spent in China and beyond that in Asia. In midstream, however, I had transferred myself to the West and to my own country, the United States. Soon, since any writer writes out of his everyday environment, I began, however tentatively, to write about American people. I became thereby someone else.

This someone else, who was now also I, for the old self, the Asian self, continued to exist and will always continue, was, I repeat, oppressed. The oppression was a determination on the part of my readers, sometimes loving, sometimes critical, to insist that there must be no other one than the one they had always known; that is to say, the Asian me. But here was the new American me, eager to explore and adventure among my own people. To provide freedom for this American me, pseudonymity was the answer. The writer must have a new name. I chose the name of John Sedges, a simple one, and masculine because men have fewer handicaps in our society than women have, in writing as well as in other professions.

My first John Sedges novel was *The Townsman*. It is a long book, a story of the West, Kansas in scene, to which state I had made many quiet visits. I was pleased when Kansans praised its authenticity. Its hero is a modest fellow who refuses to ride wild horses, be a cowboy, shoot pistols into the air, kill his enemies, find gold in any hills, destroy Indians or even get drunk. He is content merely to become the solid founder of a town. The novel was well received by critics and sold to some tens of thousands of readers. It thus proved itself as a successful first novel by an unknown writer.

Four other novels were published under the name John Sedges, and guesses became rampant as to the author. No secrets in this world are kept forever. Someone always knows and tells. And my two selves were beginning to merge. I was by now at home in my own country, my roots were digging deep, and I was becoming increasingly familiar with my own people. The protection of John Sedges was neither so necessary nor so effective as it had been. In Europe the John Sedges novels were openly sold as Pearl Buck books. I was moving toward freedom. The shield was no longer useful.

So John Sedges has served his purpose and may now be laid away in the silver foil of memory. I declare my independence and my determination to write as I please in a free country, choosing my material as I find it. People are people whether in Asia or America, as everyone knows or ought to know, and for me the scene is merely the background for human antics. Readers will still be the critics, of course, but I shall hope and strive to please and to amuse. Why else should books be written?

I confess that I was proud of *The Townsman*, prouder than I have ever been about any book of mine when Francis Hackett, then the brilliant literary critic of *The New York Times*, gave it a glowing review. True, he guessed the author when he said the novel was "in the English tradition from George Eliot to Pearl Buck," and so proved that he knew at once who John Sedges was, but I was still proud when the Kansas City *Star* said that the novel had certainly been written by someone who had lived a long time in Kansas, since no one else could have written such a book!

So much for Jonathan. I am glad you like him. I rather like him myself.

Where were we in this conversation? The scene around us

has changed. The car is moving swiftly along the highway in central Florida. I have never been in this state before, having had enough of the semitropics elsewhere in the world, I have always told myself. Yet, all unexpected, here I am as a result of meeting you.

Our relationship at first was one of work, you the teacher, I feeling very inept as your pupil. Then the relationship changed and we became partners in a common cause. How, I wonder, did I discern in you the dynamo for whom I had been searching for three years, to work with me for the new, the lost, children born of American servicemen and Asian women? For that matter, how did I discover the children? I went to Japan to work on a film and one day, indeed the first morning after my arrival, I saw a child with Japanese features, but his eyes were blue and his hair brown.

"What child is this?" I asked my Japanese friend and guide.

With diffidence he answered me, ending with the sentence that fell on my heart.

"We believe there are some two hundred thousand of them. It is impossible to know the number. Usually their births are not registered anywhere. Their mothers are ashamed of them."

"And their fathers?" I asked.

"They are gone," he replied simply. "They are Americans."

I was silent, but thereafter wherever I was I searched for this child, on the streets, in orphanages, in village and town. Ah, there were many, many, and though many died, many lived.

That same autumn I went to Korea at the invitation of the Korean people, and there the child was again, wandering on the streets, lost and alone, segregated in poverty-stricken orphanages, swarming around American camps. One face among the countless in my memory is the bright intelligent face of a fourteen-year-old boy, in a miserably poor orphanage. He had had a severe attack of poliomyelitis, and he was almost entirely paralyzed. Yet he did move about, on his stomach, wriggling in the dust. When he lifted his head out of the dust, I saw a beautiful bright face, an American face, and he asked me questions about America, which were translated for me to answer. I could see he was thinking about his American father. What could I tell him? I evaded the truth. I went away quickly, and I find him with me always.

When I came home again I knew something must be done for these half-American children, who are our blood relatives through our sons and brothers. They must be given a chance to grow into good men and women, a benefit to the lands of their birth. As usual, I tried every source for help.

TFH: And as usual, not being able to get anyone else to do a thing, you did it yourself. This tour is a good example of just that. After you formed The Pearl S. Buck Foundation for these children you decided the world must know about them, and not being able to accomplish this in any other way, you decided to go out and talk to as many people as you could get to listen. I have wondered many times, if I lived in your beautiful house with your comfortable income, secure after a lifetime of successful work, would I be so driven as to get into the back of a car, as we are now doing, our belongings in a luggage van leading the way, and travel thousands of miles, cocktail party after cocktail party, ball after ball, speech after speech, just to tell people about the children? I have heard many people, great and not so great, introduce you and talk about you on this tour. They gush adjectives like a Hollywood gossip column. They call you a great humanitarian, a brilliant novelist, a mother, a gracious lady, and then they begin to recite titles and awards. All that they say is true but I feel they really miss the truth about you. Since I've come to feel I know you so well I have decided that really you are just an indignant storyteller. In fact, I think everything you've ever accomplished stems from indignation. You are gently but firmly determined to voice your opinion on a subject or a situation, and not finding a chance to do it otherwise you write it into a story. Long ago you couldn't get an adoption agency to place a mixed-race child because they couldn't match parents. You became indignant, saying it was stupid to base parental love on race, creed or color. In indignation you started your own adoption agency, and judging from the success of Welcome House, you were right to do so. Everything I've seen you do began in much the same way.

PSB: Meanwhile, always searching for the person who could help me to begin this particular work, I was watching you, the way you worked, the way you organized yourself and everyone around you, the influence you had on your associates, everything that you did and said:

"Is he the man the children need?"

This question I asked of myself and I alone was the one who must answer it. Yet I am never quite sure of such aloneness. For I do ask for guidance in whatever I do. Call it prayer? Yes, perhaps! When I knew that it was I who must be responsible for the Amerasian children since I could find no one else to assume the responsibility, I sent out a call into that Space, that Otherness, which I see only darkly and not yet face to face.

If I must undertake this work, I said, I cannot do it alone. I am not fitted to organize, to administer, to be an executive. I called for help. Someone must be found. I must find someone. But who? And where? I had considered many young men, for this work is a long work and the man must be young. He must have integrity, he must have the skill for organization, he must have a personality that can draw people toward his cause—and therefore to that cause he himself must be dedicated. It is not often that one finds the capacity for dedication.

So while you were reading my books and asking your own questions I was asking, too, and waiting for the conviction, for or against you, which for me would signify guidance.

TFH: I was so busy trying not to sound like a Gestapo agent with my endless questions I didn't realize for some time that you were asking questions of your own. When I became aware that indeed I too was being quizzed and I began to wonder how it was that you were so interested in my crazy life. I tried to explain the somewhat strange philosophy of my mother when she and I had the long talk years ago that resulted in my leaving home while so young. The first time I went out on my own I was only twelve. I returned after that only occasionally for schooling of sorts but always with my mind dedicated to my own art. Moving often, a few months here, a few months there, I lived in a total of forty-four states in seventeen years. My education therefore is of the practical variety. It consists mainly of all I have learned from experience with people. I fully believe that about ninety percent of any success in life depends entirely on the efforts of others. It was because of this basic belief that I concentrated all of my efforts on learning how to interest others sufficiently in the things I wanted to accomplish so that they would help me. A good example of this type of study is the seven years of dramatics it took for me to lose my Deep Southern accent. I did this on good advice because I discovered that people listened only to how I was speaking rather than to what I was saying. I think my well-developed "Yankee" speech now is one of the main things that my family, all staunch Southern Baptists, resents about me, next to my interest in the dance. Though my mother and father did not share the feelings of the aunts, uncles, and cousins, it is, I'm sure, the prospect of "hell fire and brimstone for eternity" that caused me to become determined to do as I wished. Perhaps my mother knew all of these things the day she said:

"You should go somewhere else, to a new city, in a different part of the country, away from all of the family, and make your own life. I think then you will be happy—and I'll help you all I can."

You can see how I would wonder what you thought and how you felt as I told you of these beginnings of mine.

PSB: The story of your life is so extraordinary that one day you must tell it yourself, in all its variety. As for me, I try to imagine what your mother felt when she sent you out into the world, still a child, to make your way alone. I am sure it was with agony and with despair. Yet how wise she was, how courageous, to separate you from an environment which could have destroyed you utterly had you remained in it! Of course it was with heartache that she sent you away and I am sure she woke in many a night to suffer and to weep. And of course you knew she was right to tell you to go to some other part of the country, away from the poisonous influences that played about you in the narrow Southern town where you were born, an army town, filled with restless, lonely young men in search of whatever life and companionship they could find with the girls there. Ah, what courage, what courage, in both mother and son! And I think it was this courage, combined with your great creative talent, which I discerned in you very soon after we first met, that led me gradually to the conviction that I had found the person for whom I had been searching, ever since I saw with my own eyes the lost Amerasian children, in Japan and Korea, and heard from others that they existed in large numbers in Okinawa and now know are also in Vietnam. In a sense you were a lost child, too, fending bravely for yourself in a world of greedy adults. Without talent, you could not have survived, in spite of courage, and this leads me to reflect upon how fortunate we are, we who are born with certain talent. Wherever we go we are directed by that which is within us. We recognize ourselves early, and we pursue our own way. We save ourselves again and again, with instinctive wisdom, and however we may fail it is always temporary, for when we face destruction we are resolute to save ourselves again, and at all costs. I maintain that this is constructive, this courage to break away, to start again, to find life elsewhere when the environment imprisons. It is total freedom that such as we must have and though we may be called ruthless, ruthless we can be when it is a matter of the spirit's survival. This is the liberating force of talent.

In some ways my own life parallels yours. I too was subjected to a narrow religious community. Yours was what is called the Hardshell Baptist, mine was Southern Presbyterian. Fortunately my parents were broader than their creed, as yours were. In the days when I had my own difficulties with the churchly powers, reproachful Christians wrote letters reminding me of my parents and suggesting that they would have suffered, had they been alive, to know how far I had wandered. On the contrary, I might have replied, had it been worthwhile, that in his time my father, too, was called a heretic. He was a great scholar, reading his Bible always in the original Hebrew and Greek. He it was, for example, who explained to me that the seven days of Creation were not really days, for the word day, he said, had been mistranslated. It should properly be translated as seven aeons. I found later that these corresponded to the seven stages of scientific evolution of the development of life upon our planet. But my father suffered the same persecution as did Galileo before him. Nevertheless, he stood stoutly by his convictions and did not yield to persecution or name-calling.

Something of this independence was his gift to me. Thus I know well the necessity to escape a spiritual prison. For a growing talent the necessity comes again and again. You have been driven from one place to another, from one job to another within your field, always seeking the place where you could work in freedom. I have moved from one world to another, living in continents and among peoples, wherever the air breathed upon me most free. Of course under necessity we have been ruthless. We have broken human ties when they bound us too close. The truth is that when a human being is in the grip of his own talent, he sacrifices anyone and everyone. This is not to say that we are not able to have friends and lovers. Indeed the sensitivity of talent predisposes us toward love, with all that this entails. We make mistakes more quickly than ordinary mortals do. But we do not stay by our mistakes. Call us disloyal, but the truth is that we are supremely loyal, we who are the gifted, but it is to our gift that we are loyal. When friends, lovers, family, try to possess us we cut the bonds, though we bleed.

How does one discover the quality of the talent? you have asked. There are lesser talents and greater ones, in varying degrees, I reply. I discern the true artist, the greater talent, in the men and women who in the performance of the chosen art forget themselves and all others in their devotion to the art. A great artist is a great performer, and he is great because he is oblivious to everything except that which he is performing. As a consequence, he is a simple person in his daily living, for he learns early to discard everything that impedes him. He has no time for roistering and time-wasting, nor for self-conceit—not if he is a true artist. He knows indeed that "art is long and time is fleeting," and he fears distraction. Nor does he tire. One never tires of the work one loves. I am convinced that fatigue is the result of inward rebellion against life. It is a deep weariness born of despair. To work at that which one loves is to live relaxed and free from basic tension. The one piece of persistent advice I give to my children is this: Know what you like best to do and find a way to make a living by it.

Herein is contained the story of my own life—and I believe of yours, too. You wandered the length and breadth of your country in search of freedom to do your work. I changed my life within and without, to that same end. Here we meet, in a common task.

TFH: As we ride along this beautiful stretch of Florida coastal highway that connects Jacksonville to Fort Lauderdale on this peaceful Sunday morning, it is difficult to imagine that there was ever a time when I didn't know you, yet it was only a scant year and a half ago that we met. I suppose I feel I know you so well because of your books and your willingness to discuss them, their characters and their creation. I learned much about you from hearing how you take one trait from this person, a dream or two from that one, a driving force from another. You blend them all with a generous dash of your own wonderful wisdom and philosophy, and from the varied parts of your own life you create a new person. You deftly breathe life into him with words and he becomes fresh, though not flesh, factual but not actual. I first became aware of this when I asked about the people in *Letter From Peking*. A woman alone, her son, her husband Gerald and his new Chinese wife, the old Chinese gentleman, all so real, in a story, and yet beautiful. I can't help asking about them again and now!

PSB: You touch a sensitive spot in a writer. Each book is the fruit of a period of growth in the writer's life, and growth is the result of experience. You know how often people ask me which of my books I "like best," and how impatient I am with this question. How can one judge which parts of one's life are "the best"?

My book, *Letter From Peking*, reaches deep into my own life, and not just mine. For example, the letter has indeed been written from Chinese husbands to American wives. The Chinese man is practical. When one wife becomes inconvenient, he takes another, and living under a Communist government a Chinese found an American wife very inconvenient indeed. The story hinges on the letter. Elizabeth is not myself and yet she is myself in some aspects, in character if not in events. Baba was created partly from the material of my father but more from one I loved and of whose long decline I wrote in *A Bridge for Passing*. Gerald is of course the central character in the book as indeed he was for a certain period in my own life. His father was American and his mother was Chinese. As is usual with these East-West people, he inherited the best of both sides. He took his height from his father but his slim grace from his mother. He had the youthful brilliance of his father but the inherited sophistication of his mother. I suppose I made my own final decision when I discovered that he loved his Chinese mother more than he loved his American father. He was his mother's son. He felt fiercely defensive for her sake when he learned that his father had first loved a beautiful English girl and had been rejected by her. On the proverbial rebound he then had married the plain-faced daughter of a wise old Chinese scholar, rationalizing this act by saying a Chinese wife would help him in his work among the Chinese people. When his wife died after many faithful years, he married rather soon his former love, by then widowed. It was at this time that Gerald—it was not his true name, of course—learned that his father had never loved his mother, though he had been good to her in his fashion.

To his passionate defense of his mother I listened with understanding but I withdrew. I am an American woman and I perceived that what he needed was a Chinese wife. He denied this with vehemence but I knew him better than he knew himself. When I had absented myself completely by going to another country, and ceasing to write—at what cost it seemed to me then—he married a Chinese. We met years later, and I saw at his side a quite plain-faced woman like his mother. Was she happy? Was he? It was a question not to be asked because it was not to be answered.

Yes, it is strange how one takes bits and pieces from one's

own life, and joins them with bits and pieces from the lives of others, welding them together through the imagination until a new whole is created. I use the word created with intent, for all is as immobile and shapeless as marble before the sculptor takes up hammer and chisel. The creative process is instinctive. It cannot be explained except to say that within the storehouse of a writer's material one's own life and experience are accumulated, too, and are chosen, as any material is chosen when it is needed. All experience is available as everything is available to the artist's creative mind. I call it creative hunger. It is an insatiable hunger for order. There is something compulsive in the artist's instinct for order. It can only be satisfied by taking disponent parts of life and establishing order through them and with them. This order is art, and talent is the means whereby it is created.

TFH: Our last trip, from Fort Lauderdale to Tampa, was made in the still of a moonlit night and writing was impossible so we indulged ourselves in that pastime we seem never to tire of, talking. It is not just talking, for endless small talk bores us both. Indeed, I can always tell when you reach your rather low boring point. A distant look comes over your too expressive face, as though you had completely removed yourself from this present time and place and had left behind the ever-courteous physical shell the world has come to know as Pearl Buck. This is the "public affairs" you. I've given the mood, if it can be so described, this name because after getting to know you I learned that the usual social exchanges bore you at once, so bored you seek your own escape. I remember your telling me that, for you, one of the most attractive things about ballroom dancing is the chance to get out of your chair and away from the well-meant chatter always being aimed at you.

For my part, I really am unable to recall when we didn't talk furiously from the moment we came together until we parted. This late evening drive was much the same. We discussed our favorite topic, talent. I recall our exchanges of viewpoint on our first few lessons and am aware of how much we have developed the subject to our mutual satisfaction tonight. I began with the firm conviction that it was determination not talent that was important and you insisted that talent was the more important. It was during such discussion that we first talked of the Foundation as we moved to the rhythm coming from the record player, practicing the required patterns of dancing. You claimed I had talent for dancing. I said not!

PSB: It is true that I began to be curious about you and with something more than my usual curiosity as a novelist. As I have said, I had been looking for a certain person ever since I made my visit to Japan and Korea. In Japan I had met Miki Sawada again and had visited her castle home, crowded with children she had accumulated, the children of American servicemen and Japanese women. Oh, the pathos of those children! I had seen them long ago in Asia, and they were called Eurasians. Then they had been the children of empire, their fathers English or European, their mothers Indian, Indo-Chinese or Indonesian. But these now were not the children of empire. They were and are the children of American men, and they are born not of imperial rulers but of liberators. Let them be called Amerasians! You remember that was the name the man in the State Department suggested, when we went to Washington for advice. I was appalled at the number of the Amerasian children, for I saw many of them not only in the safety of Miki Sawada's home but wandering the streets and hanging about the American camps.

I had not planned to accept the invitation to Korea that autumn but Miki Sawada urged me to go, because there were many more such children in Korea. So I went, and I did see them there, beggars and wanderers and orphans in orphanages. It was then that I determined to make them part of my life. That is, I became involved. All this you know.

There is a notion among some literary critics that a writer should never ecome "involved" if one is to be an artist in his work. I repudiate this idea, and I have my witnesses. Charles Dickens was deeply involved, indignant always about human wrongs. Tolstoy dedicated himself to the practical expression of his ideals. Victor Hugo became so involved that he was compelled to leave his country, and was it not Zola who devoted himself to civil rights for Dreyfus in France? The list is endless. Nor did these great writers involve themselves for the sake of material. They forgot themselves, they dedicated their talent. Sometimes they even sacrificed it. They were totally involved. I myself never purposely seek involvement, preferring indeed to detach myself from so-called "causes." Thus I have always declined to enter politics, and thus I take joy in living in my homes, summer and winter, remote in countryside and mountains. I like the pace and tranquillity of family life. I have seen enough of human disturbance. Yet I could not take shelter in those dear haunts when I returned from Asia. I could not forget those new and lost children. Their faces, so piteous, remained in my memory. I recognized the old compulsion. I knew I would have to do something about them. Thus I was involved, and the plan for a foundation to which I would give my own name began to shape in my mind. The search was on.

I knew I could not head such a work myself. It must be a

man, a young man, with organizing skills, with complete integrity and, as I have said, with the capacity for dedication. For him it must be a job, but also a lifework. A cause? Yes, but not a charity. These American-fathered children are not a charity, but a responsibility to be shared with Asia. Where could I find the right person? I confess I never thought it would be you until the idea occurred to me one day when I realized that you were organizing everything and everyone about you and so skillfully that it was painless for those concerned. I wondered, and then delayed. You had lived a wandering sort of life, yet always within the framework of organization. You had sought education in your way, fitting yourself under the guidance of experts in the very areas that I needed help. I did not decide at once, you may be sure. I inquired, I examined, I observed. And I waited.

TFH: Our lessons continued and I became aware of a deep-rooted determination in you to do exactly as you pleased whenever you pleased. This is almost a ruthless quality in you and yet there is a basic contradiction. You accept whole-heartedly the rules and disciplines necessary to acquire what-ever it is you want to learn. You are not satisfied with anything less than excellence. Thus you were perfectly will-ing to comply with the standards of good dancing. You learned cha-cha and merengue, your least favorites, as readily as your more favored waltz and tango. This was strange to me. In all of my experience I had not taught anyone who never said she didn't like this or that. I knew you didn't want to become known as "Pearl Buck, Jitterbug," yet it was only necessary to explain once to you how swing develops quick footwork and single balance more quickly in all your dances, and with your "Patience thy name is Pearl" look you set about learning the art of swing without a single complaint. When I remarked how refreshing your attitude was, discipline joined talent in our discussions. Perhaps it was your inner discipline that made you so easy to teach. It is first necessary to become master of one's likes and dislikes, and thus win the battle of whim, before one can ever master the art of dancing and enjoy the real beauty of it. With you it was easy, for discipline and determination are the way of your life. Many times I've heard you talk with groups of young people about cause and purpose in life and I've heard you take them right back to the day of their birth, indeed the very moment, to explain this inner will to win.

PSB: Of course art itself is the strictest discipline. The notion that one sits at ease while writing a book, for example, is sheer ignorance of the process. One's whole life is disciplined in preparation for the practice of one's art. For the body is the medium and the tool and it, too, must be disciplined if it is to perform. Haphazard ways of living not only destroy the body, they destroy the talent. Irregular sleep, irregular hours, wasteful habits, all must be changed to an orderly way of life if one is an artist. It is fashionable to think that an artist is a bohemian. The truth is that bohemians are never true artists. True artists work. They are jealous of their time. They are prudent in their food, knowing that a headache can ruin a precious day. I saw as I came to know you that you were now mature enough to know this for yourself. Were you or were you not the one? I took another step toward decision.

As for the birth bit, as you call it, it is an example of how and where a writer sees illumination. I faithfully read scientific magazines, as you know—not those dealing with applied

sciences, since it is theoretical and abstract science that interests me. In one such magazine I found a description of the
human being in birth. It was written in physical terms but my
mind seized upon the symbolic aspects. For the human being
the moment of birth is equaled in daring and determination
only by the moment of death. The transition from one stage,
one phase, one atmosphere, to the next is bold and swift. It
might be called wholly instinctive except for the critical
moment when the will must decide for life. Otherwise the
being dies.

What a change it is to be born! Through all the prenatal
months the human being has floated in a warm protective sea,
enclosed and safe, spared shock and effort. Sleeping, the
creature hears no voice, even his own; sees nothing and no
one, his eyes closed; feels no touch upon his new and sensitive
skin. Suddenly, without warning or understanding, he is
ejected into an entirely new environment. He feels rough
hands and stuffs pressing upon his tender body. He chokes,
his lungs are full of liquid. He must breathe or die. But to
breathe is a new adventure. It demands an effort of will. For a
brief moment he hangs between life and death. No one can
help him. It is he who must decide whether to lapse into the
inertia of death or draw breath for life. Solitary and alone, the
human being makes the great decision to live. He breathes and
gives a loud cry. For the first time he hears his own voice. For
the first time he hears the voices of others.

Again and again as he lives his life he must repeat the
performance. Again and again he must, always alone, make
the decision to enter into a new and wider atmosphere. Who
knows? Perhaps death itself is no more than this.

Had you the will to move out of the security of the dance

world into the atmosphere of a wider world? Were you the one?

TFH: By now your lessons had become the highlight of my life. Many times I said that everything I've ever learned is from others and it is true that much of my education has come from the brilliant people I have taught. Yes, I've spent many interesting hours teaching pupils from various professions—the wives of doctors, lawyers, stockbrokers, golfers, bowlers, or of professors of this or that at some college. All people like most to talk about that which they know, so in drawing someone out I learned first to talk about that which my pupils knew best. Then, being gifted with a rather quick mind, I absorbed each bit of information that might be useful to me in working out my own life. In you I found a wealth of variety and I felt much the same as a prospector must feel when he strikes a new vein. Of course, as we danced, I used the obvious springboard to conversation, your books. You seemed perfectly willing to discuss any and all of them except *The Good Earth*. At first I thought this strange, but now of course I can easily see why. About ninety-nine percent of the hundreds of people you meet rush up and gush, "Oh, Miss Buck, I so enjoyed your *book!*"

Poor Wang Lung and O-Lan—may they rest in peace! I also know now that although I did ask the usual first question, at least I had the grace to tell you first that I knew I shouldn't ask. Indeed, I've learned that no one should ever ask an author:

"Which, of all your books, is your favorite?"

PSB: Incident! We have just stopped for a cup of coffee as we travel the highway here in Florida. The restaurant is handsome and well equipped. We sit down at a small table, you and I, the chairs are comfortable, the atmosphere pleasant. It is still early in the day and not many people are about. A neatly dressed waitress takes our order and immediately reappears with hot coffee. We are about to continue our conversation—how endlessly we talk, you and I, bridging the years by our interest in our different worlds! Suddenly a blare of raucous song shatters the peace. Someone has dropped a nickel in a juke box. I am seized with resentment. I demand of you:

"Why should another person force me to listen to what *he* wants to hear?"

"Why indeed?" you reply. "There ought to be another slot for your nickel, so that you could stop the noise."

We sit in our own silence, drinking coffee, as the hideous, senseless voice grinds its way to the final foolish plaint of calf love, and I ponder your question.

It is true that I have no favorites among my books. Each represents a period of my interest and involvement in life. *The Good Earth* is the result of long impatience with a certain group of young Chinese, the Western-trained elite, the sons of rich families, sent abroad to gain degrees from American, European or English universities. Such young men, and the fashionably modern intellectual class they created, totally ignored the eighty-five percent of their compatriots who were peasants. The Chinese peasant is a notable human being. He is stubborn, independent, hard-working, intelligent. He longs to know how to read.

"Not to be able to read is to have the eyes of my spirit blind," an old peasant once mourned to me.

So easily might the brilliant young men and women have helped their peasants! I dare to say that had they done so,

Communism could never have laid its dark hold upon China. I remember a manuscript that once came to my hands. It told of the experience of two young American pilots whose planes had been downed by Communists in the Chinese inland. They were interned in a Chinese village where they observed the ways of the Communists who were trying to win the people.

"How much better we Americans could have done it," one young man wrote. "The Communists give the villagers the simplest of medical and educational help, but it could have been much more had we given it."

This manuscript was never published, although I thought it should have been.

I remember how often in my time I besought young Chinese intellectuals to go to the villages and open schools and clinics. They preferred, however, to crowd into the cities where they could have modern plumbing and see Western films. I place blame squarely upon the selfish elite in China who did nothing to make the peasants' life more tolerable. It was for the voiceless peasants of China, therefore, that I wrote *The Good Earth*. The book fulfilled its purpose and I lost interest in it.

As for the film made from the book, I remember the magnificent performance of Luise Rainer. She moved, looked and spoke like a Chinese peasant woman.

"How did you do it?" I inquired of her once in admiration.

She explained that she chose a young Chinese woman on the set and followed her about, and learned of her. But of this film I remember most clearly that I did not go to the opening in New York. Why not? Because I feared I would not like it and might have to pretend that I did. I went to see it the second night and sat quite alone in the front row of the balcony. After the picture was over, I heard one man say to another:

"What do you think of it?"

The other considered and then replied, "Well, I'd ruther see Mae West."

No, I have no favorite book, since, as I have said, each book represents a phase of my life and growth. Different countries, different people, choose the book they like best. Somewhere, somehow, each book finds its own readers.

TFH: Philadelphia and those first hours we spent together seem worlds away now while we ride along the Sunshine State Parkway this morning on our way to Orlando and another group of people, another situation, another ball, literally and figuratively. That's one of the amazing things about us. We have enjoyed each moment we've spent together, even though, at times, all we could enjoy was each other's boredom with other things. Maybe it's because it all started with pleasure and humans seem to have a natural tendency to expand what they already have to include new things rather than forfeit the familiar for something strange, enjoying a new experience most when surrounded by things or people grown used to. As your knowledge of dancing increased, it was a joy to see the pleasure you gained from perfecting a school figure. Some of your observations were amusing to me, for example, when you excused yourself saying:

"Thinking with my feet is a new experience for me."

Then, with an expression of absolute delight and excitement, up would go your hands to the required position, and with fingers waving of themselves, off you went to master the solo execution of the material for your next test.

PSB: It is quite true that dancing has given me joy. I live a concentrated sort of existence, giving to each demand a single-minded and profound attention. The writing of a novel is of itself a concentration. The deep and solitary preparation, the devotion of thought and feeling to the development of the characters before the finality of writing, place a total demand upon the writer. I have few relaxations. Music, perhaps yes, but the hours of practice necessary if one is to achieve mastery sufficient for enjoyment are again a concentration of thought and energy. Nor can I find relaxation in games. I have no competitive spirit and therefore care nothing about winning. This lack of interest makes the game meaningless.

Dancing, however, provides something entirely new for me, and I find it enchanting. It requires discipline of the body, a physical skill which I enjoy, combined with a new sort of mental discipline. Moreover, there is companionship, for one does not dance alone, at least in ballroom dancing. How often have I come to the studio feeling weary, and how often come away restored! All problems slip away when one is dancing to the rhythms of music. This is not to say that I like all dancing, however. I refuse the unbeautiful and angular grotesqueness of the twist, for example. It is tolerable only when performed by the very young, preferably the adolescent. It changes the adult into someone ridiculous—at least to my eyes.

Nor do I care for the cha-cha. I perform it with some ease now, but it is too monotonous for my interest, nor do new gyrations relieve the unchanging beat that has no sweep. The rumba has a certain grace, but the tango and the waltz give me the satisfaction of style and elegance in movement. I shall continue dancing as long as I live.

TFH: We talked of everything in our lessons, as each book I read led you to tell me of some experience from your own life. *Pavilion of Women,* for example. I'll never forget how excited and pleased I was when I finished that book. I could hardly wait until your next lesson to ask you about it. How flattered I had felt when I first mentioned it to you in the course of some conversation, before I had read it, and you said:

"I've never asked anyone to read my books, and I've never asked anyone what they thought of them, but I'd like you to read that one when you get a chance, and tell me what you think of it."

Of course I immediately dropped the one I was reading and embarked on the life of Madame Wu after forty. On your next lesson I expressed my single thought to you.

"You told the world a great deal more about Pearl Buck through Madame Wu than you would ever tell in *My Several Worlds* as Pearl Buck."

PSB: Yes, I remember that remark and I remember being secretly staggered by your perceptiveness. I suppose I wanted to know what you thought about Madame Wu because then I would know what you thought of me! Essentially, hers is the story of any woman of superior intelligence. She dreams of ultimate human communication and companionship which, because she is altogether woman, can only be with a man of intelligence at least equal to her own. She hopes for an intelligence even higher than her own because, by the very nature of her being, she knows she will continue to grow. But, like Madame Wu, she may find herself married to a man to whom, in her scrupulous mind, she owes a duty. How she performs that duty makes the universal story.

Madame Wu once caused me quite a problem, however. A

young American woman, weary of rapid childbearing, decided she would "do the Madame Wu," as she put it, with her own husband. The result and confusion in her family and community would have made another long novel. But I shall never write it. I simply reflect upon the responsibility a writer has for what he-she writes. It is the same responsibility that falls upon the scientist when he discovers and creates. Is he responsible for the use that others make of his work? He cannot be, for if he is thus burdened he will not have the freedom necessary for the exercise of his talent. So with the artist in any field. The loss to humanity would be incalculable were individual talent stifled by responsibility for what others may do. Therefore I will not be responsible for Madame Wu!

TFH: As I have said, I discovered early that your boring point is extremely low. At regular studio parties and functions I watched with amusement as you squirmed and fidgeted while some woman expounded, say, the qualities of her favorite dishwashing detergent. What welcome relief comes over your face when someone rescues you by asking you to dance! On the other hand, I've also watched when your rescuer happens to be a man not very well versed in the art of dancing. I can almost see your artistic self leap out and dance about the room on one of its explorations as your physical being continues in its trap, you with your abstract expression, trying to decide what is expected of you as you struggle to follow! We talked for awhile of how strange it is to watch life, as though from afar, involved but not a part of it.

PSB: This habit of mine of abstracting myself from the present scene returns to your thought, it seems. Does it disturb you somehow? But it is quite true that I have a secret place to which I withdraw when I am surrounded. When did I begin doing this? When I was a child, a white child surrounded by curious, half-admiring, half-amused brown faces. I saw myself then an object rather than a person and I withdrew from time and place so that I should not be compelled to the position of "the special one." In a way this early experience has helped in my later life. When I first came to my own country to live I was already called famous. I became again an object instead of a person, and once more I found myself withdrawing into my secret habitation. There I am alone. No other enters.

And yes, my boring point is low, perhaps, but I am not sure that I am ever really bored. We were talking of talent, you and I, of which you have your share, and so, may I say modestly, have I. We agreed that talent is a liberating possession, freeing us to pursue many paths. You said that talent is simply a super-energy which can be used in various ways. Thus, you said, you are convinced that you can do anything you wish and do it with excellence. You take this for granted and, somewhat to my surprise, you are not in the least conceited. In this you are quite Chinese, although you have never seen China. It is merely that you are a superior person and you accept the fact. How do I know? Because I am like that myself! Nor have I ever seen a superior talent that did not know its own worth, and this in all humility. The superior person is humble, knowing that what he has is given him by grace, and not by any merit of his own, nor by striving. We are responsible for the use to which we ourselves put our talent, however, and neglect or misuse is, I take it, that sin against the Holy Ghost of which wise scripture speaks. But for me the Holy Ghost is the life-force itself, which we do not understand, although all creation comes from it. To be given creative talent, therefore, and not to use it, or to use it for evil ends, this is the sin.

Here I sit, in the car, ruminating over such thoughts—nay, call them convictions—and writing them down before they slip from me, while you saunter among bags of sun-ripened oranges and small palm trees at a roadside stand in Florida, on our way home from a tour of benefit balls. It is time, is it not, to explain why we are here and how it all came about? Let us proceed. No, wait a minute—I have one more point to make. It is not that my boring point is low. It is simply that people like you and me know the value of time. The span of a life is not enough for the full use of that which we have been given as our share of cosmic creative energy. For us time is treasure, never to be wasted. It is not that we are bored. It is that we are impatient to be about our business. I am impatient. Are you or are you not the person I am seeking?

TFH: I really don't know how to tell of how the Foundation first started unless it grew out of our talks about the Welcome House Ball in your barn. Yes, I think the first mention of it was as long ago as that. My job in that affair was different from what it has been since. I was trying to get the ball organized and still be a part of the show. Well, it was a great success and somehow during all of this we began to talk of the children of American servicemen and Asian girls who could never come to this country for adoption. It seemed to me even then somehow unfair that here were these children, related to us all, without any chance for anything other than a life comparable to that of the very lowest form of humanity.

Still, it was foreign to me personally as I'm sure it must be to most Americans, and my real interest at the moment was to do my work well and to continue your lessons.

Invariably, however, as we would cha-cha or waltz away we would fall into conversation about this problem. It was after the ball in your barn that we began to consider the possibility of a really big affair in downtown Philadelphia. I discussed it with the manager of our school, and he seemed to think it a great idea, and so a ball was born with great enthusiasm out of which was to grow The Pearl S. Buck Foundation.

PSB: When did it begin? I remember a certain evening and a certain meeting when a good Pennsylvanian expressed the caution to which I am so well accustomed and with which I have my own ways of coping.

"It's too big a job for us," he said.

I saw you leap to your feet, as straight as a flame of fire with your shining red hair and blazing dark eyes. I remember your very words:

"We will do it ourselves, then!"

I liked your temper, I liked your fearlessness, your so intrepidly flying in the face of the Establishment, and I liked your declaration of independence. I made up my mind at that very moment to keep an eye on you, for some purpose not then clear to me. As I write these words I see the narrow tower of Cape Kennedy soaring into the eastern skies and I am reminded of another man, who once upon a time was young and fearless in his time and place, as you in yours, and as determined. There is something in common here.

Before I can define the quality we are in a town and it is Malabar. Why is there a Malabar in Florida? The only

68

Malabar I know is a hill in the city of Bombay, India. On the hill are the Towers of Silence, that solemn place where people of Parsi faith expose their dead to waiting vultures. Those dark and dreadful birds swarm down out of the sky and in ten minutes, I am told, a corpse is stripped clean of flesh and the skeleton is bare. The explanation for this custom is that the earth, air and water are among the sacred elements and since a dead body is polluted, it may not be disposed of in any sacred element. But more than ever why Malabar in Florida? No answer, no answer, as once again upon our homeward journey the car glides along the road beside the sea, where tall gray herons wait.

And Malabar passed by, why is there Melbourne? It belongs in Australia, surely, yet here it is, Melbourne, Florida, U.S.A. Question upon question, as East meets West! Wanderers and travelers must have named new cities for old cities they had loved, and somehow the mingling of old and new put me in mind of the children again, the half-American, lost in the streets of Japan and Korea or in poverty-stricken orphanages.

I had kept my thoughts vague at first, for I was busy enough and did not want, either, to begin a big new job. Weakly I had suggested to other agencies the necessity of doing something special for the children of American servicemen and Asian women. They are the casuals of war and Occupation, these new children born without family, and their faces had haunted me, their look so lost. None had responded. The lost children continued to be born and to grow out of childhood. So, at last, reluctantly, compelled by the memory of the children's faces, I knew I myself must act—and delayed, mainly because I could not think of the right person to help me, someone young and dynamic, capable and dedicated. I was looking for this person, thinking that when he was found, I would begin. Were you the one? I kept delaying the answer to my own question.

Would you be able to understand the need? Would you want to understand? For that matter, how could I be certain that you were the right person? These were the questions that were restless in my mind as I set about fulfilling my plans.

TFH: We left your house that evening, the manager of my studio and I, the two of us determined to show the world what could be accomplished with energy and enthusiasm. We stopped at a little country inn, nestled quietly in the trees at an intersection a few miles from your home. There we drank good imported beer and discussed the coming events, mapping out our plan of action. We declared that our ball was going to be so big that none of the hotel ballrooms in Philadelphia would be big enough so we had better hold it in Convention Hall! It was a mad idea but, fed by our enthusiasm, it grew and was decided upon then and there. I'll never forget your answer later when a well-meaning society matron said:

"My dear, you can't hold a charity ball in Convention Hall. It has no prestige!"

You drew yourself up to your full height and said, "I take my prestige with me."

Our regular studio staff meeting the next day was begun with the announcement of that Convention Hall decision, and so began the long series of events that led up to the concrete move to establish the Foundation. In the six months that followed I grew completely frustrated with people saying:

"It can't be done."

"I care about the children but I can't buy or sell tickets."

"I care about the children but I can't help you."

A million and one reasons and excuses, but to me the fact remained that if such people really cared, they would do whatever was necessary to help with the problem.

PSB: Indignation is one of the greatest motive energies in creative life—perhaps the greatest. Is love not involved? It is indeed and it is basic, for indignation springs from love, violated—love of a person, love of humanity. Had I not loved children, would their faces have haunted me? Had you not loved them, would you have cared whether tickets to a ball were sold?

TFH: Slowly your concern and mine moved toward meeting and I began to consider leaving the studio. I didn't know where I would go or what I would do but I knew I would leave. I am not a social worker and I felt this excluded me from working for the children. What then? Would I go to another studio and start over again with a new situation, a new group of students? I didn't want to do that, yet I knew I could not continue where I was. Such was my frame of mind on Christmas Eve of that year as I waited for you to come in.

It had snowed all night and was still snowing that morning as I trudged my way into the studio at 10:30 to prepare for our eleven o'clock lesson. My old friend and dance partner was already there working on the studio books and the new secretary employed for the ball was working away on her duties. I remember there was some discussion as to whether you would make the twenty miles from your farm to the studio through the snow. It was my opinion that you would because I hadn't heard from you. It looked as if I was wrong but at eleven five I heard you coming up the stairs. With all this indecision in my life I was a little depressed, I'll confess, at the prospect of facing another Christmas with no definite roots and nothing permanent in my life. I knew you planned to go to Vermont with your girls on the day after Christmas and I couldn't have blamed you if you had stayed home on this Christmas Eve. Therefore I was somewhat relieved when you came in. Time had begun to pass slowly between your lessons and I really wanted to see you before you went away.

Our lesson started much the same as any other lesson that morning and it was during the second fox trot that I asked:

"Have you made any New Year's resolutions?"

A question innocent enough in itself but I certainly was not prepared for your answer.

"Yes, I've decided that, immediately after the first of the year, I'm going to my attorneys and set up my Foundation. I'd like you to go with me. I want you to know how it's set up, for I'd like you to be in it on an equal basis with me. I'd like you to be the head of it."

PSB: Yes, I remember the snowy Christmas Eve. I went that day to the studio, my head full of plans, and my determination firm. The decision was in the tradition of my life. I never decide any step quickly. Much thinking and dreaming go into the creation of any plan, whether of an action or a book. I begin with a definition of what I want to accomplish. The goal, the end, must be clear and defined, so that every step, every means, is justified and in accord with the end. This I believe is necessary for accomplishment, lest in unsuitable or unworthy means the end be lost and the goal never reached. Thus, during all the day preceding that snowy Christmas Eve I had been defining and planning. As I have said, I knew that I must find a person capable of achieving the goal. More

72

than once in my life I have needed such a person. When I know I have found him—or her—I choose quickly, but at the right moment.

How did I know that the person I was looking for now was you? How does one know the moment of decision? By the same intuition, based on knowledge, that one begins the creation of a book. By a strange process that can only be called creative thought one arrives at the moment and recognizes it. Thus I had for many weeks been observing your talent for organization and leadership at work. I knew by now that the studio gave you far too limited a scope for your abilities. I understood your frustration and discontent. You were applying to this small area effort, energy, imagination, that needed world scope. I had a plan that spanned continents, east and west. The children of America and Asia are world children. Never mind how they are born or at what level! They are the result of the meeting of two great cultures. Properly received, recognized, welcomed and educated, they can be the leaders of tomorrow's world. Either they will be that or they will be international rebels and criminals. They are the most important single group of human beings alive today. They continue to be born and will continue, since it is obvious that, for the unforeseeable future, American servicemen will remain stationed at various strategic places in Asia. Nor can we expect Asian peoples to feel concern for these children if we do not. And what lovely children they are— lovely and not to be wasted!

My mind was full of such thoughts that morning of Christmas Eve. Suddenly with a clarity of which I have been aware at other moments of great decision in my life, I knew you were the person whom I had been seeking for these children.

Almost without knowing it was I who spoke, I heard myself say the words you have repeated. I shall never forget the look on your face when you heard them, unbelieving, joyful, doubting, wondering—something of everything I saw.

TFH: The expression on my face? I must have blanched. I was stunned. Never could I have imagined such a thing. Here was a possibility of having everything I'd ever wanted, and yet it was much like walking in darkness. I had no way of knowing where the next step would lead me. All I could do was stammer:

"I shall have to think but however I decide, I want you to know I am greatly honored."

Thus began the endless hours and days of trying to make up my mind. Of course I wanted to do it. To be associated closely with a person of your greatness for many years? Anyone would want that. Yet for me it was not reason enough. As a fringe benefit the association with you would be wonderful, but I couldn't change my life and dedicate myself just to a person. A person, however great, is still temporary. Were these children really important enough to me for me to give up my life as I had known it and dedicate the rest of it to a problem about which I really knew nothing? It was a question only I could answer. I was widely traveled in my own country but I had never been abroad and had no desire to go, really. Besides, working with such a famous person does put restrictions on one's life. Not that I had ever done or wanted to do anything I would be ashamed of, but suppose I should ever want to? Think, ponder, fret! What to do? What to do? I discussed it with every one of my closest friends in my efforts to decide. They all thought it was wonderful, but what it always boiled down to was that they thought you were wonderful, which is true, but, as I've said, that's not enough. Days stretched into weeks and still I could not decide. Then Kim Christopher came into my life. I'll never forget that day you came in and brought a letter from an American woman in Korea. You went straight to your bench as usual to wait for your lesson to begin. I came over to greet you and you said:

"Here is the letter I told you about over the telephone."

Here is the letter:

"Il San, Korea

"DEAR MISS BUCK:

"How does one answer a letter received from someone who has been an idol to you since adolescence? Someone whom you have admired and revered as a human being and a writer since the day you took *The Good Earth* from the high school library shelf? One cannot really, and do it adequately. Not any more than one can adequately express thanks to someone who has helped to guide and direct your life to its final purpose, God willing, the Orient and the damaged, unwanted child.

"All I can do is give you a crudely done charcoal sketch inspired by the blessed face of a half-American baby boy nobody wanted, and the miserable words coming from a bleeding heart at his death.

"For a barren, unwed woman beyond the years of 'high on a windy hill,' love and desire, this work is not a sacrifice but a glory. *Letter to Peking* is my favorite of all your books. To me it is not a novel but sheer gentle, lovely poetry. *The Living Reed* has helped me so much to understand this poor, bartered, little nation and its wise, attractive people.

"Bless you, and to meet you personally would make me very, very happy."

When I read that letter and poem any doubts I had left me and my final decision was made.

Here is the poem:

> Who killed Kim Christopher?
> I remember the day he came
> Tied on a stranger's back.
> Hamster cheeks,
> Blue eyes huge with wonder,
> Skin like brown cream.
> A happy, silly smile
> On a trusting, "love-me" face.
> Who killed Kim Christopher?
> He had no name
> No birth date
> No record of existing.
> His life story?
> Birth,
> Abandonment,
> Pneumonia,
> Death,
> Time?
> Six months.
> Who killed Kim Christopher?
> The father who gave him life in a moment of lust?
> The mother whose race could not accept him?
> The monsters who made a war,
> Or the snug and safe who ignored him?
> Who killed Kim Christopher?

Some day I must meet the writer of this poem and tell her what great changes she brought about with her pen.

And while I am quoting these words which helped to make

our decision, let me quote too from an article in the Los Angeles *Times,* January 8, 1964.

"Sidetracked in the Christmas mail was this haunting letter to the Times from Capt. W. L. Jones of an MP unit stationed in Korea.

" 'My story, though not new, is still worth telling, and I beg your indulgence.

" 'I am stationed in an area called Ascom City. Near my compound is an orphanage with many children. However, there are twelve who are more destitute than the rest. They are of GI fathers, without any known relatives or outside support.

" 'On Christmas Day this pitiful group was brought to the unit for dinner and gifts purchased by members of the company. It was a frightening sight at first because one got the impression that these children were left in this oriental country by American parents who had forgotten to count heads before returning to America. Because of their American or western physical appearance they are segregated from the other orphans.

" 'These twelve children live and sleep in one room approximately 12 x 12 feet. They have no bed, they sleep on the floor and, as far as I could ascertain, have two blankets. The temperature as I write this letter is fourteen degrees above zero.

" 'At dinner one little boy was asked to take off his jacket. He refused, then bashfully opened the top to show he had nothing else on. Another little fellow ate all the ice cream he could hold and wrapped the rest in a paper napkin and put it in his pocket, as he said, to eat later.

" 'It is impossible to relate the suffering these little children endure. I hope those who read this story will find it in their hearts to send any old clothing, blankets or toys to these helpless children.

" 'They include one boy 11, two boys 9, two boys 7, three girls 9, two girls 7, two girls 5.' "*

PSB: The long road winds through the Carolinas as we write. Last night we stopped at a motor lodge, the four of us—you, Jimmy our photographer, and the chauffeur and I. It was in a small town in North Carolina, and I supposed we would pass the night, you remember, peacefully unknown. But no, I was recognized in the office when we went to pick up our various room keys. A tall heavyset young man approached me, his eyes pleading, and asked if I would give him even a short interview for his newspaper. I hesitated, for we had been driving all day.

"Please, please," he begged. "If you only knew—you see, no one important ever comes to our town."

I was touched, and I stayed a few minutes to talk with him.

"What do you want to know?" I asked.

"Could you say something about our state—something you found interesting?"

I told him then about Dr. Rhine at Duke University and how upon retiring he planned to set up his own center of research into extrasensory perception. This young American had never heard of Dr. Rhine, and when I understood he had not, I told him how the people in other parts of the world

* Reprinted by permission from the column by Matt Weinstock, Los Angeles *Times*, January 8, 1964.

knew and respected Dr. Rhine and how the Maharajah of Mysore had come all the way from India, hoping to meet him. It had happened several years ago that I had an invitation from the Maharajah of Mysore, then visiting in New York, to have luncheon with him at the residence of the Indian Consul General. I accepted, knowing of the Maharajah's interest in philosophy. When I arrived at the appointed hour I found a large tranquil young man, overweight but with a magnificently handsome head. He barely spoke for the half hour before luncheon, nor did he trouble to talk during the meal. I was in despair. Why had I been invited? After lunch I made one final effort.

"Your Highness," I said, "what do you wish most to see while you are in the United States?"

His calm face lit. "I wish to see Dr. Rhine," he said.

A prophet has honor in other countries, if not in full measure in his own!

I too had long wanted to see Dr. Rhine, not from any interest in the occult, but because I believe, as he does, that there is a rational explanation of every phenomenon. We went thither, you remember, on a bright autumn morning during this journey and found him to contain in himself the elements of true greatness—that is to say, he is modest and grateful for every talent. He is a scientist, with a scientific approach to his research into extrasensory perception. We had a long and satisfying talk. As usual when I meet greatness I waste no time. I proceeded at once to inquiries into his techniques. Of these he himself as well as his wife have written in several books. It is not my business here to describe anything except himself. I discerned in him the cosmic energy.

Something more I discovered. Like all others through whom flows the cosmic energy, this man is neither understood nor appreciated at his full value, or so I guess from his wistful manner as he spoke of his meeting the age of retirement. As if genius can retire! He plans to go on with his work, as genius always plans.

The young man listened, enthralled, as I spoke of Dr. Rhine, and I discerned in him the same hunger that I discern in most of our young people—a hunger to meet greatness somewhere. Ours is an era singularly without heroes. Our habit of debunking and decrying our great individuals desiccates us spiritually, I think. "Where there is no vision, the people perish."

I left the young man after a short while, but you stayed for an hour and more. And you told me this morning that you had discovered that in this little town there is a military post of some thirty thousand marines, many of them newly returned from Korea!

It is another of our increasing number of coincidences, which do not happen by chance, I am beginning to believe. Anyway the young man will write a report of his conversation with us about the Amerasian children, and somewhere among the crowd of young marines there will be response. It was like you to seize the opportunity even at the end of a long traveling day to continue the work to which we are dedicated. Even before that snowy Christmas Eve I saw in you the capacity for dedication in whatever you decide to do, large or small, and your determination for full accomplishment. It is a trait all too rare these days. And I think no one has it except the born artist, whatever his medium. We have a passion for perfection in whatever we do. Call it dedication!

At any rate, because of you thirty thousand marines will possibly take thought of the children they may have left behind them in Korea.

So to return! I left for Vermont after Christmas, that year now past, and with me my four daughters, they to ski, and I to sit at my desk at work. It was difficult to keep at it, I remember. In the first place, the snow-covered mountains made a glorious vista under a sky of brilliant blue. In the second place—only I am not sure it was second—I thought of you and wondered what you would decide. If you were the right one for the immense task ahead you would know it and accept the responsibility it offered, heavy as it was. If you declined—well, then for once my intuition and judgment would have failed. I could only wait out the slowly passing days alone in my house, so quiet until darkness brought the children home again.

When we met after the holidays, you had still not decided. I knew I must not add a word of persuasion and I did not. When you said that you had to be sure you were not coming for personal reasons, I was happy. I wanted you to come only for the work itself. Otherwise you would not find joy and fulfillment in it. But somehow I knew you understood that, you so independent in all that you do, and I waited without urgency.

That was the day when the letter, the sketch, and the poem came from Korea. I have never met the woman who sent them and now I do not even know where she is. Again it was the coincidence which surely does not happen by chance. I too was moved by what she had written. I knew I must show to you what she had sent me, because it expressed so deeply the children's need. Profoundly concerned though I was with their need, I purposely had not made an emotional appeal to you on their behalf. I did not want you to base your decision on your emotions. Yet apparently that was what decided you finally. How strange that she, unknown, should appear in our lives when each of us needed her most and having accomplished this without herself being conscious of what she had done, that she should slip away again, forever unknown!

TFH: Once my mind was made up, everything in my life began to take on a new appearance. People, places and things shifted to new positions in order of importance. I tried to retain my friendships, which I had thought to be deep and strong. Yet one by one these persons whose opinions I had valued and whose support I counted upon, dropped away. They became part of the past. It still seems incredible to me that I could have moved into a town and lived there for two and a half years and come out with only the same three friends with whom I went in. I had settled myself into a close, warm relationship with a number of people who professed to think much of me and to be interested only in my future happiness. I must say that it was a sharp awakening to discover these people as they really were. I found them to be interested only so long as I could move in their circles and be of value to them. This is human, I suppose. We are all guilty of thinking first of ourselves.

There is only one relationship that I miss sometimes. I had become extremely fond of the studio manager, a big, warmhearted, overly generous man, and his quiet even-tempered wife. I recall the many hours we spent together, the trips we took and planned to take. I began to feel a great sense of loss, although my scope broadened and my world enlarged. I've noticed before that, as a circle of friends expands and one's world grows larger, the people who once were close either stay with the hub and remain in the center or they cling to the rim, trying to keep the circle small, like Emmet Kelly's light. The ones who cling to the rim move farther and farther away. They grow smaller and smaller in relation to the whole until they no longer exist. My true friends have stayed close to my hub for many years. I look out beyond them and am faced with a great well of loneliness that can be filled only with work. Is this well not inevitable where there is talent?

PSB: It is inevitable and only talent can make it bearable. With a work to do and the talent to do it, however, one can cope with personal loneliness, for talent fulfilled brings the deepest content that an individual can know. Perhaps it is the only way to assuage the loneliness every human being must endure at times—and perhaps, basically, all the time. One's first impulse is to assuage by establishing relationships of friendship and love with other human beings. It is a youthful impulse and sooner or later life teaches us that love dies and most friendships change with time and propinquity. Sometimes it is we ourselves who outgrow the ones we once loved and depended upon. If you have three upon whom you can unfailingly count, you are fortunate. I would like you to believe that there is now a fourth.

TFH: You never tell the world anything about yourself, only what you have learned. People love you for this but I am sure that there are thousands of people who would like to know how Pearl Buck learned all these things and how she became so wise. You wrote a book of your times, *My Several Worlds,* and it is called an autobiography. It isn't really, as even you are quick to say. No, you tell of yourself in other ways. You take experiences from your own life and credit them to some new person you have created and weave a novel. Why is it when you are given a chance to relate an incident of your own life you evade?

PSB: Yes, I am the recipient of love, and this I have been from time to time throughout my life, and from various persons, for which I am deeply grateful, by which I am profoundly moved, but to which I cannot give myself wholly because I am already committed, not to any person, but to the work that for me is life. Yet I am by nature a warmhearted woman, I think—no, I know—and I have yielded many times to the impulses of warmth which are always in me. However much I may love, nevertheless, and do continue to love, for I have—what shall I say?—an almost unrealistic passion for loyalty, I am not able to give my time and attention, undivided, to anyone. Yes, I have my firsts and above-all-others, but I wander my own paths, nevertheless. I have before me today, for example, by one of those chances which in our lives are never quite chances, a poem written for me by a very dear and unchanging old friend, a man upon whose love I have depended, without the slightest yielding of my life, these many years. The poem is dated August 30, 1964. It is now the day after Christmas, months later. I must have tucked the poem into a corner of a drawer in my desk here in my Vermont home. We come here for skiing after Christmas each year, but this year I wanted a different Christmas, as you know, and so came before the holidays. Today, a foggy gray morning and the mountains outside the window hidden in mists while you and I sit here writing back and forth in this curious fashion, I discover the poem. Here it is:

I have heard your voice
Reaching across the distance
A distance not our choice,
But puzzling Fate's insistence.
　　Yet, since we're far apart
　　We know the mystery:
　　The one-ness of our heart
　　Defying history.
Shall we thank this perverse fate,
Compelling love to roam,
Yet keep inviolate
This spot thy heart's true home?
　　For God himself is still:
　　All power is effortless,
　　The wellspring of our will
　　To touch, to love, to bless.

He wrote it on a summer morning because I telephoned him that I could not meet him at an appointed place. Why? Because—because I had a book to finish and above the delight of meeting was the deep joy possible only when the ending of a book comes clear. I create without knowing the exact end, and when at last I see it it is like walking up the mountain through the mists to see the crest suddenly carved against the sky. This is happiness and one can achieve it only in supreme loneliness. Yet—and here is life's paradox—I am as aware of loneliness as any human being can be, and in one sense there are no compensations for what I missed that day last summer when I said I would not go to meet the one who waited.

I suppose that the influence of Chinese culture is part of my being. In the China I knew I absorbed the Chinese attitude toward friendship. There friendship was an indissoluble bond.

When two or more persons decided to be "blood" friends, no change in the individuals concerned could break the friendship. It was for life. This custom was ingrained in me. Once a friendship is accepted in the deepest sense of the beautiful word, nothing can break it.

I have twice owed my life to such Chinese friends. The first time, properly speaking, it was to a friend of my father's, for I was only a small child. This friend was a Chinese gentleman of great dignity and high learning, the Viceroy of the province of Kiangsu where we lived. How did he save our lives? The year was 1900, the year of the dreadful Boxer Rebellion, so called, when the Empress Dowager, in old age and desperation, decided to rid China of all foreigners by murdering them. She sent an imperial edict to the Viceroys of each of China's eighteen provinces commanding that all white people be killed. Our Viceroy friend was horrified. He knew how foolish and dangerous such an edict was, and into the edict he had received he inserted a negative before he reissued it, making it say that white people should *not* be killed. Thus we were saved.

You remember the big Chinese chest now in the library of the Foundation headquarters in Philadelphia? It stood for many years in my study, first in my own Chinese home and then in my American home in Pennsylvania. Well, it was the Viceroy's chest, which he designed and built for his official files, and it was given me, in his memory, by his daughter, who was my friend.

The second time my life was saved? I have told that story in *My Several Worlds* and I need not repeat it here. Merely to remind you, I will simply say that when the Communist armies of the Second Revolution marched in triumph down the Yangtse Valley and reached the city of Nanking where I lived then, they attacked all white people. The date was March 27, 1927. Several of us were killed that day, but we lived, I and my family, because Chinese friends saved us at the risk of their own lives. Yes, in China the bonds of friendship are eternal and in a strange tragic fashion the deep rift today between China and the United States is a result of the Chinese tradition of friendship, which we do not share or even understand. For a hundred years the Chinese thought of Americans as their friends. We had helped them in famine and flood, we had never seized their land as other nations did. How often had I, wandering where no white person had ever gone before, been questioned as to my own nationality! When I said, "I am American," the reply was invariable.

"Ah, America is good."

At the end of the Second World War, when Communists seized power in China, we repudiated that country by cutting all ties. I am sure this caused consternation, anger and despair among the Chinese. In their opinion, how can friendship be broken merely because of a change in government, based on a change in ideology? They cannot understand us any more than we can understand them. How different the world might have been, had there been mutual understanding! But about friendship, perhaps they are right. At any rate, their love has been turned to hate. Today a whole generation of Chinese has grown up without seeing a single American, or hearing anything good about us.

Yet I remember that two or perhaps three years ago I received a letter from a woman in Denmark. She and her husband had only just come back from their business in Shanghai, and she brought me messages from Chinese who said to her in secret:

"Tell Pearl Buck to tell Americans that we do not hate them. We remember our old friendship."

TFH: Let's go back to our story. I'll never forget the day of Joseph Levine's premiere of *Yesterday, Today, and Tomorrow*. That evening I began to know you as you really are. The film and party afterwards were interesting. Life simply went on with no apparent connection with the past. I met, for the first time, other people with whom you are associated— your business partner and the director of Stratton Productions, for example. I wondered how you, of all people, came into the gaudy world of motion picture-making, in any way other than by writing books. The idea of you trapsing all over India making a picture with multitudes of people simply didn't fit with the you I had known. How and why?

PSB: As to how and why it was simple enough. In the first place, I am always ready for something new if it expands life. Adventure for adventure's sake? No. But adventure for the sake of new outlets, new vistas, new experience—yes. Thus I am always interested in new and better ways of communication. Books are primary, of course, but pictures have always enticed me, a visual approach in depth. I suppose the immediate incident was a television show. My book, *My Several Worlds*, had just been published and *Omnibus* asked me to let them do an hour's show from the book. It was something new, and I accepted the invitation. A script was prepared, a director appointed. He was Tad Danielewski. The name was new to me. He asked if he could have a talk with me. I agreed and a week or so later he and his wife drove down to the country to see me. I scarcely remember that visit—an alien young man, American but Polish-born, a pretty Polish wife, expecting their first child. What I do remember was his careful and courteous effort to discover my wishes for the program, his anxiety that all should be to my taste.

We began rehearsals, in due course, and I liked the way he directed, graceful and fluid. He was, I perceived, an artist in his own field. He understood and evoked the atmosphere of the book. Scenes were performed against a background of Chinese passing across the screen, a frieze of living people, and I in the foreground, reading from the book. So it went, smoothly and with faithfulness, until about an hour before we were to go on the air. Suddenly there appeared a man I had not seen before, a short sandy-haired person of curt manners. He was the power, it seemed, for he did not like what the director had done. In a few moments, by a few orders barked in a rasping voice, he removed all that was graceful and beautiful from the show.

"It's not commercial," he said.

How often do I hear that phrase now that I am indulging in my avocation of picture-making! Where did I first hear it? I did not hear—I saw the words years ago in a letter written me from a literary agent in New York. I was then living deep in the heart of China, and just beginning to write. Would the agent act on my behalf in the United States? No, he wrote back. Why? Because the American people were not interested in China. In fact, Chinese stuff was not "commercial." I went on writing it, nevertheless, and it has been commercial, in my case. Commercial—what is it? It means will people be interested enough to buy? My experience is that people's interests are far deeper and wider than we give them credit for.

I went away from that first television show deeply depressed. It was, so far as I was concerned, a failure. What had been truth, artistically expressed in visual terms, had been debased to a rather silly, obvious performance in which I had not felt at ease. I had forgotten the director as I left the studio. Suddenly I saw him standing in a corner, fists clenched, face turned to the wall, and very grim. I knew exactly how he felt but I did not speak.

Weeks later he came to me with a proposal to make my story, "The Big Wave," into a television show. I accepted, and wrote the screenplay myself. The show was a great success and my reward was the headline: PEARL BUCK TELEVISION SHOW A MASTERPIECE. Forgive me if I boast a little! I am not given to it, am I? But this was a new field and I enjoyed succeeding in it.

We did one more television show together, the director and I, and it was my story, "The Enemy." The famous and beautiful Japanese star, Shirley Yamaguchi, played the lead. I was happy with the show and again had fine reviews.

Then one of those strange, senseless shake-ups occurred in the networks. The imaginative and talented Pat Weaver was replaced and with him departed his imagination and his creative genius. I wrote no more for television, on the advice of my faithful literary agent, and Tad Danielewski resigned when the change took place.

Our friendship continued, however, our thoughts moving in the same direction, and one day he proposed that we form an independent production company. We consulted my husband, who urged me to go into the venture, knowing my interest in the field, and, alas, perhaps realizing his approaching death, as I did not, could not, would not.

"It will give you wider interests," he said.

It was here in this very house that the decision was made, here where you and I now sit at work in the Green Mountains of Vermont. It was a clear day, I remember, a summer afternoon. Stratton Mountain is my front yard, the lesser mountains rolling away from its flanks, and Tad Danielewski stood by the wide windows in the living room, looking out.

"Let's call our company Stratton Productions," he said. "Symbolic, isn't it? We lift our eyes to the heights."

That was how it all began and that was how I became involved in the gaudy atmosphere of motion pictures and have continued to be involved to the extent of several pictures. And that was how you and I happened to be driving together to New York to a premiere of one of Joseph Levine's films.

TFH: We got home late the night of the premiere but the next morning I was up early to survey what I had done and to plan what next to do. In the preceding month I had set up a desk in my small apartment, designed our letterhead, leased a typewriter and had already begun to make a few contacts. We had our first two members of the Board of Governors of the Foundation. In principle we had agreed immediately that we would seek people of the highest status in every field of endeavor on the Board of Governors because these American children so badly need status. Joan Crawford was our first member. I've long been an admirer of her work and as we entered her apartment in New York one afternoon in February I was naturally quite shy. We were armed only with the clipping from the Los Angeles *Times* to show the need of the children—the one by Matt Weinstock—and at once the great star was moved to say, "Of course I'll help you in every way I can. Now let's see who else can be of help."

She thought of Art Buchwald, called him in Washington, and an appointment was set for us to meet with him and that was our start. She was—how shall I say it?—she was simply her wonderful self.

Art Buchwald, when we met him, was equally as willing to help us and so our Board was formed with a membership of two. Eddy Robinson, an acquaintance of mine, had promise of becoming very useful to us, and, at my request, he became our third. Soon after that he gave us our first contribution in the form of the carved wooden water buffalo now standing on the Chinese altar table in the foyer of the Foundation, under Chen Chi's painting of *The Good Earth*. At the opposite end of the table are the two fighting cocks we bought in California—remember? You fell in love with them, although they are Italian, not Chinese!

PSB: Cocks are the same the world over, and I fell in love with them not because of any country. As a matter of fact, I wanted them because of a happy day I spent in Manila not too long ago, but before you and I set up the Foundation. Tad Danielewski and I were on one of our film projects and we had stopped in the Philippines, I not only for the sake of films but also because of James Yen's Mass Education work. I have written elsewhere of James Yen, my friend of many years. He was the only Chinese modern intellectual I have ever known who really tackled the problems of the Chinese at the village level. He himself was reared in a scholar's family, and like all Chinese intellectuals, ancient and modern, he was remote from his own people. He had come to Yale for his doctorate, and after receiving it, had accepted a job in France, the period being that of the First World War, when there were thousands of Chinese peasants digging trenches. Labor was China's contribution to the Allies.

These men were pitiable, for they could not read or write and so could not communicate with their families. In the midst of writing and reading letters for them, Dr. Yen devised a technique of teaching them a thousand of the most used characters and thus enabling them to write and read within limitations. Their gratitude moved him to decide to devote his life to teaching peasants when he returned to his own country. There he devised a fourfold system of aid for villages in agriculture, health, literacy, self-government. He was spectacularly successful but was compelled to leave when a Communist government was set up. After observation, he decided to set up his work in the Philippines, where he has been similarly successful. One can always tell whether James Yen has been at work in a village. It is clean and prosperous and the people look happy and hopeful. I have long been on Dr. Yen's Board of Directors and hence my interest in this great man and his unselfish work.

Where was I? Ah yes, in Manila! Well, there came a day just before we continued our long journey when work was done and we could take a day off. It was hot and humid, summer was upon us, the hotel was temptingly air-cooled. I resisted temptation. I had been too busy to see anything of the city, and I did not want to lose the opportunity.

"Let's sight-see," I suggested to my partner.

"Not me," he said firmly. "I shall spend the day in the swimming pool."

I kept my disgust to myself, and without informing him, I

hired a cab and a driver who spoke English and spent the first part of the morning in seeing the ruins and sights connected with Filipino history, especially those connected with Rizal. Toward noon my driver asked if I had ever seen cockfighting. I had not. He suggested that we go to see a famous cockfighting theater. I agreed. He told me then that cockfighting was illegal in Manila but we could see it in Quezon, not far away. To Quezon we went. There for two hours I watched the fascinating sport, leaving betting to my driver. We came out ahead, as I remember. It was a noisy place, I also remember, for the hall was crowded with men—so far as I could see I was the only woman—and they shouted their bets.

What I remember most clearly, however, is the way the owners of the cocks coaxed and encouraged their birds. They stroked them and praised them with words of enchantment. I sat in the very front, next to the raised stage, and thus could see everything. And what impressed me, too, was that the little brown scrawny cocks always won the fight and the big white handsome cocks were only dazed when they were vanquished, as though they could not understand what had happened to them. I hope there is no symbolism in that! Anyway, that's why I loved the two fighting cocks we bought in California. Now they are a continuing reminder of the happy hours I spent in Quezon.

TFH: I faced my desk one Tuesday morning and I knew we had outgrown my small apartment and our humble beginnings. There was also the problem of my own time. I had never used a typewriter, for example, and my painful "hunt and peck" forced me to take hours on a single letter. I had already asked the ball secretary if she would come with the

Foundation after the ball. She had agreed, but that was more than a month away. I could not wait. I called her again that day and asked if she would do my letters at home if I got a dictaphone. She agreed and one problem was licked.

We had been out looking at large houses to hold our offices, you remember. Well, now there was a possibility of a large estate being given to us in the Chestnut Hill section of Philadelphia so I knew that any office space would be temporary. But where to go? Should we locate ourselves too far from the city? Better not to decide yet! I knew I wanted to be out of Jenkintown and away from any unpleasant memories there, so I leased a dictaphone and boarded a subway into Philadelphia. Within two hours I sat in a two-bedroom apartment at the Drake Hotel and that was our first office. I called you and told you what I had done. You approved, so I then called my housemate and asked him to bring my typewriter and some clothes when he got off work that evening.

With all those details out of the way I sat down and began to dictate. That was our first real day of operation. I remember laughing to myself at the mental picture of the Executive Director of The Pearl S. Buck Foundation, sitting in the middle of a large hotel apartment, with nothing but a dictaphone, calmly carrying on business. I understood then for the first time your need for roots. I felt for the first time in my life, too, a need for permanence. I knew our job would take many years and I needed a place to spread out and work, undisturbed. I was already learning from you how to organize my time and how to get things done. I learned, for example, that you use force of will when it is necessary to set yourself to a task and get it done. I began to try to pattern myself after you in this respect. What is the old adage? "You can't argue with success!"

PSB: I liked the way you resolutely set yourself to work after the decision was made—no regrets, no time wasted. Long ago I learned that nothing is more futile than regret. And work is the great assuager. Of course neither of us knew the full magnitude of the task we had undertaken. I had arrived at the concept of the task by various stages; first, by setting up an adoption agency for the mixed-race children; second, by realizing after visiting Asia, where American men are stationed in great numbers, that adoption in the United States would never solve the problem of these unwanted half-American children; third, by the conclusion that something must be done about it, preferably by someone else but if that were not possible, then by me, with such help as I could get.

The more we discussed the task, you and I, the greater we perceived it to be. Thousands of half-American children, born displaced, forgotten by their fathers, rejected by their mothers' people, surviving as best they can in hovels, ditches, culverts, around camps, in poor orphanages, yet fine children capable of being good citizens if they have a chance, a blessing to both their countries instead of burden and disgrace! Sensible people would have given up the whole problem but we have a trait in common—we never give up after we are convinced. Not once have we considered giving up the Foundation we have set up as a means of life for these new children. Our first necessity, however, was to define our purpose, not only for ourselves, but for others whom we planned to approach. Hence the Statement we wrote. It was as much for

ourselves as for anyone else. Somehow it gave us reassurance
to have it down in black and white.

Statement by Pearl S. Buck
on The Pearl S. Buck Foundation

First, let me say that this is the only agency to which I have
ever given, or will ever give, my own name. I have done so
because, after fifteen years of observation and experience in
the field of lost and needy children, I am compelled to the
conclusion that the most needy in the world in our present
age are the children born in Asia, whose mothers are Asian but
whose fathers are American.

Until the last war there were so few of these children as to
be negligible, but since the war there have been many and
they continue to be born wherever our men are stationed. I
am well aware of the fact that there are many needy children
here in our own country, but also there are many agencies to
look after them. In Asian countries this is not true. Moreover,
the problem of the American-Asian child in Asia has little to
do with the economy of the country. In Japan, for example,
where there is great prosperity, these children are still se-
verely discriminated against mainly because they have no
families. In the family-centered societies of Asia, if one does
not have a family, there is little chance of adequate education
and of jobs. There is of course the natural prejudice between
races, to which we in the United States are accustomed, but in
our own country. This prejudice is between Americans,
whereas in the Asian countries these children are considered
"foreigners." Had it not been for the dedication of Mrs.

97

Miki Sawada in Japan, who has devoted her life and her fortune to the welfare of the American-Japanese children, the situation there in that country would have been very bad indeed, for the number of such children is large because of the Occupation, and indeed they continue to be born, too, since we have military bases there. I am no prude, as you know. It is inevitable that such children are born when we send young men far from home and family. The fact has to be faced, however, that they are born, and that we Americans are partly responsible for them. As an American myself, I cannot believe, moreover, that it is good for American prestige for our half-American children to grow up illiterate and without the opportunity that other children even in Asia have. The result can only be a criminal class of persons of whom the Asians will say, "See what the Americans have left behind."

In a country like Korea the situation is worsened because of the poverty of people and the economic problems resulting from the political and geographical division of the country. These children continue to be born now, it is estimated, at a rate of some one thousand a year. I visited Korea rather recently and took time to discover the status and conditions of the American-Korean children, and the inescapable conclusion I reached after discussion with Western and Korean agencies, as well as with many Koreans, and my own daily observations in the quite complete tour I made of Korean cities and countryside, was and is that the American-Korean children are in a hopeless situation. It makes one feel very strange, I can tell you, to have a beggar child put out his hand for a penny and look down, not into a Korean face, but into the eyes of a child unmistakably American!

Through Mrs. Sawada in Japan and through Korean agencies in Korea and through Welcome House, Inc., here in the United States, the latter an American agency founded fifteen years ago for the adoption of children of Asian-American children in good adoptive families in the United States, many Amerasian children have been adopted. My recent visits to Asia, however, convinced me that adoption alone cannot solve the problem. We cannot at best bring more than a relatively few of the children to the United States. What is to become of these half-Americans left in Asia? Can we Americans afford to let them grow up a criminal group, a constant burden in the Asian country where they happen to be born because our military forces must be stationed there?

After facing this as an American with long experience in Asia, I determined to set up a Foundation which would have my name and to which I intend to devote my own efforts for the rest of my life. Its purpose is simple. We will begin with Korea where the need is greatest. We plan to station there an American representative of the Foundation, preferably a young man and his wife, chosen for their ability and their dedication. It will be their duty, working with a group of Koreans, to discover the American-Korean children, wherever they are, and to see what the conditions under which they are living are, child by child. We do not plan to set up institutions or orphanages. There are already enough of those in Korea and in them are many of the American-Korean children who are usually segregated, I am sorry to say. We will work with these orphanages not to give the American-Koreans more benefits than the others have, but to bring to them the same level of food, clothing and opportunities for education. We intend to help to get them jobs when the time comes.

If possible, however, we will try to keep the children with their mothers. Where the mothers are camp followers, we will try to help them to get work and make a decent home for the child. In Korea especially there is a very strong feeling against a woman who has a child out of wedlock. Whatever her station, when this happens she loses her job and is usually cast off by her family. This compels her to prostitution and camp-following. It will be our effort, always with the help of Korean friends who are already deeply interested in our Foundation, to help this woman to regain some sort of status through our interest in her and our efforts on her behalf. The total purpose of whatever we do will be to integrate the American-Korean child into Korean society by helping him to become a good citizen in the land of his birth and therefore a benefit to his fellow citizens and not a burden and a curse. It is my hope that *because* he is partly American he will be a better citizen. The grounds for this hope are quite practical. I have had experience with hundreds of these children in my lifetime and nearly always the racial mixture produces a child superior to both sides of his ancestry. With education we can well be proud of our share in him, and he will be an honor to us instead of a disgrace.

I hope you will see the importance of this work and will help us to do it.

I thank you.

TFH: I understand fully our need for funds. Fifty thousand half-American children in Korea alone! These were the figures sent in from the Korean Government. Here I insert a letter from a Government official in Korea:

"Now, coming back to the statistics, more than 6,000

children have been so far placed overseas. Let's say 1,000 of them were full Koreans. The remaining 5,000, then, were half-Americans. Almost everybody concerned with these children, both experts and laymen alike, agree that children adopted constitute only ten percent of the total. If this were true, we can then infer reversely the total to be 50,000.

"There are other factors, which can support this argument. There are some fifty or sixty thousand U. S. soldiers in Korea. However, not the same ones are staying all the time. They are rotated so often that their gross number is well over 80,000 per year. On the other hand, established figures indicate that there are more than 80,000 prostitutes in Korea. Let's suppose this were correct (though I believe it is more). Of course, not all GIs are mating with these girls, but their companionship rate is higher than before. Unlike wartime soldiers who have to move from one place to another very often, the after-ceasefire soldiers are stationed in one place for 18 months or so of their stay in Korea. Somewhat stable as they are, chances may be higher that their weekends are spent with these girls who are roaming around their camps. At any rate, although not all GIs are playing with these girls, all of the 80,000 girls are and must be living on their 'business' with these boys.

"Now, fertility of the Korean women, especially of these girls, is very high. Birth rate is estimated at more than 50 per thousand, per year. This rate is probably lessened by abortion and stillbirth rates. Thus, it can be estimated that some 2,400 half-American babies are born alive per year to these 80,000 girls. When this is multiplied by 20 years (since 1945), the number will be nearly 50,000. It is noteworthy moreover that this estimate is based on a lower assumption—low birth rate and high abortion and stillbirth rate, and there were more than 500,000 GIs in Korea during the Korean War.

"My social work field began after college at a job on the Population Division of Korean Bureau of Statistics, and later I taught at a university in Seoul. Thus, I can claim myself as a demographer as well as a sociologist. A controversy over the number of children under consideration can be endless, unless there is a census taken to determine an exact number. However, my 'hunch' as a demographer is that there are more than 50,000 such children now living in various parts of Korea."

Such figures, multiplied by unknown totals in other Asian islands and countries where our men are stationed, compelled me to realize that we needed money and help. Out of this need the Benefit Ball Tours were born. I suppose it was a natural thing for me to reach into my past experience for help. I knew that many dance studios would give at least one ball each year, for they were already contributing in this way to other charities. If we could get the proceeds of half of these affairs for the Foundation we would have the start we needed. But how? I consulted a personal friend I had in the business, he who is now a member of our Board of Directors. We had discussed the Foundation with him before and we both liked his ready, quick response to the problem and his enthusiastic flow of ideas on the subject. He offered to use his position to help us all he could. This he did.

PSB: I don't know what I expected a young man in the dance business to be, but this regional director of dance studios was like any promising young businessman. He arrived at my house for a weekend of business discussion with us, you remember, bringing with him his attractive young wife and their little girl. I confess it reassured me to see so conservative and decorous a family group. My old Pennsylvania farmhouse has had many visitors, but this was my first from the business world of the art of the dance.

We talked of the Amerasian children and of our responsibility for them, since their fathers are our own sons, brothers and even husbands. Yes, sometimes they are husbands. More than once I have had a young wife approach me quietly at a moment when I was alone in a crowd.

She asks the question I expect. "Is it possible for you to bring us a particular child in Korea?" Or it may be Japan.

"Do you know where the child is?" I ask.

"Yes. He is with his Asian mother."

"Is she willing for you to have him?"

"She thinks he should be with his father."

We exchange looks. I ask the final question.

"Is the father your husband?"

"Yes."

Her eyes brim with tears that she turns her head to hide.

"But he's ours," she says.

"I will try," I tell her.

Sometimes she is not successful at this hiding of tears. It is too much for her.

"Why?" she sobs.

I make the usual excuses, which are valid—loneliness, boredom, the necessity for some relationship to life when one must live in the presence of death imminent, the inevitable detachment from all that one has known, no end in sight, which means desolation of the spirit. She listens and sometimes comprehends.

It is the very young ones, however, for whom I feel the deepest compassion, the boys who have never known the comfort of love which includes companionship, the ones so young that they must cope with their own powerful impulses, the young men between the ages of eighteen and twenty-five, who cannot assuage the fire that nature pours into their veins. In the fearful simplicity of military life there are few diversions. Mind and spirit yield to the flesh and the body wins.

There are other reasons, too, but they lie very deep in our American culture. They are hidden in the complexities of the relationship between our men and women. Ours is not a matriarchy. Women here do not sit in the seats of power. This being true, they rebel in ways both conscious and unconscious. They assert influence by independence in their own lives. Much has been said about the strangulation of mother love. "Momism" is the coined word. My own observations, however, contradict this definition. I think American women do not love their men enough. Generalities are an abomination, but I believe, generally speaking, that American men abroad would not fall so easily into love with foreign women had they not been deprived of love here. I am not speaking of physical sex. That is easily come by and may have nothing to do with love. By love I mean that deep devotion which truly puts the other person first even in sex. I think American men give more of their love to their women than they get in return. Women, with inner rebellion smoldering in their vitals, are capable of having various primary objects for love—themselves, their children, their houses, their clothes, their amusements, their hobbies, their causes, their personal professions. They are not to be blamed entirely. Or are they? No, I think not. They are only in the first stage of realizing that equal rights demand equal responsibilities; they hesitate to face this frightening but inescapable truth and yet it must be faced before it can be accepted and dealt with. Caught between fear and inevitability, women seek a return to the past. Alas, there can be no return. In panic, women think not so much of love as of security in marriage.

"She wants to marry and she's looking for a man"—how often one hears it said, and how much is conveyed therein of what is wrong between men and women in our free society! No, I must conclude that it is lack of love which sends our men so easily into the arms of welcoming Asian women. The result is these thousands of half-American children.

TFH: You are now speaking on a subject about which I feel very strongly, as you know. I wish I could disagree with you but I cannot when I remember my own earlier years in an Army town right here in the United States. Seeing young attractive American girls of the type next door selling their favors to young-looking servicemen rather than having healthy "boy-girl" relationships gives one cause to wonder. How can we possibly expect more from those boys when they go overseas? Remember the young men in Pensacola?

PSB: I do remember, and they had much to do with my conclusions as I have just given them. Pensacola is near great military camps where thousands of young men are being prepared for service abroad. We saw them everywhere on the streets, in groups, in pairs, alone. One evening, you and I came downstairs ready to go to the ball. We were a few minutes early and so we sat in the hotel lobby. Both of us saw the young sailor boy slouched in one of the big chairs. Somehow I knew he was not waiting for anyone. He just had nowhere to go.

We had the same impulses, you and I, to take him with us to the ball. You went to him and asked if he would like to go.

He leaped to his feet, the car arrived, and we went. Somewhere, somehow during the evening we picked up nine more young men, sailors and soldiers. They found a table near the head table where we sat, and now and again we went over to theirs, and it was fun for all of us. They danced and forgot themselves and when we were ready to leave, long past midnight, they left with us and we fed them at the hotel before we parted. Only for the night, however, for during the next four days they were always with us.

I remember one incident, particularly, which for me was significant and led me in the direction of the thinking that I have tried here to express. It was the next day, at a restaurant where we had gone to have luncheon, the boys with us. You had to leave on some errand immediately after we had eaten, but the boys lingered and I stayed with them. I sat listening to their talk, for they did talk of the most private personal matters. They were worried because they had had no letters from home, not for a long time. They were worried about their families, to whom, it was obvious, they were deeply attached. They loved their parents, especially their mothers—and it was the mothers who had not written to them, not for two months, not for four months, one not for almost a year. It was incredible but true. These women did not really love their sons. They were busy with their own problems, their own lives, and they did not consider how lonely these boys were. When I expressed surprise, the eldest shrugged his shoulders. He was all of twenty-three.

"It's rough," he admitted, "especially for these kids who love their families. Me—it doesn't matter. I've never been close to my folks."

Bravado, to hide a wound made long ago! Is it any wonder

that when these boys go to Korea or Vietnam, or to other Asian lands where they are sent, they fall easily into a relationship with some gentle girl who has been trained in the philosophy that it is the duty—and the privilege—of a woman to love a man and to consider first his comfort and well-being?

TFH: We are ahead of ourselves. Let's get back to our beginning in Philadelphia. Even then we realized that we were fast outgrowing my makeshift headquarters at the Drake. We talked much about the house in Chestnut Hill and then you expressed your desire to have the Foundation in Center City Philadelphia. I listened very carefully, for I had made up my mind that your Foundation was going to be exactly what you wanted it to be above all else. You cared enough to give your name to these children and I intend to see to it that it is used exactly the way you yourself would use it. Hence it was decided that we would not take the estate in Chestnut Hill but would locate our own house in town.

You have said before that you hoped I considered you as a fourth friend. Well, I don't! This is a difficult thing to explain but a friend has to be a person separate from one's self and in my mind we are not separate. We have created a work together and in relation to that work I think of us as one and the same person, two sides of the same personality. In my desire to have everything exactly the way you want it I have tried to train myself to think out a situation the way you would, to react as you react. In its own way the Foundation will stand as a living example of the way you do things. I have no wish to use the Pearl S. Buck Foundation as an outlet to express my thoughts and beliefs but yours.

When you told me you had always dreamed of having the

Foundation in Philadelphia's historic Center City, I started the endless trek through town houses. It had to be a house, for I knew that your current four teen-agers would soon be going away to school and you would be left alone in your country home. It was my hope that then you would center your activities in the Foundation and spend most of your time there. Also, I feel that all of the things you cherished from China belong to the American people and should be housed where they can be seen. Your Chinese desk at which you wrote *The Good Earth*, the Peking rugs from your home in China, the Nobel Prize medal and citation, all of your awards and degrees, your original Chinese seal that you had when you were a child, the family Bible in which your birth is recorded, your piano and so on and so on for hours. To me, all of these things belong to the public as a part of the history of American literature and they should be kept together in one place where children, one or two hundred years from now, can look and say "That was hers."

PSB: You are fond of saying that you don't know what an executive director is or should be, but you immediately proceeded to be executive and to direct with your usual purposefulness. Your technique is infalliable. You define your goal and you move straight to it, eliminating anything and anyone in your way, and all this so briskly and pleasantly that you have assembled a group of fellow workers who are willing and happy to follow your leadership. This is an achievement. You have already done something far beyond my expectations. I am glad you see the headquarters of the Foundation as a place which involves my life. You are quite right. I am involved with the whole world, and now especially with these children, who express in their very being the philosophy which is the heart of my life and my work. I believe that humanity is one, not the same but in its infinite variety One. I am happy to have my few treasures, such as they are, a part of the central house. Somehow, in this way, the widely divergent periods and experiences of my life, so unusual in its own way, are gathered together into the house which is designed to serve these new children of the world.

Why Philadelphia? Well, the reason is simple. I love that city and I love its people. I enjoy New York and have had a semi-life there for a number of years, as you know. But Philadelphia is heart's home. There is something stable here, and kind and—yes, conservative and even conventional. Unconventional as I can be sometimes, my family roots, paternal and maternal, are in conservative, conventional people. I come of old stock, pre-Revolutionary and steadfast, but capable of surprising new adventures. My father, for example, lived a wildly adventurous life, yet I never saw him dressed except as a gentleman of the Victorian era, complete in white shirt and stiff wing collar. He preached to crowds of so-called "heathen" in cities and villages of inland China but he wore the same frock coat and black trousers, neatly creased, that he wore when he preached to American Christians in Richmond, Virginia. In our home on the banks of the Yangtse River I was reared as strictly as my brothers had been reared in our family and sent far away to an America I did not see until I was nine years old and then only for a few months. Our family life was old-fashioned, courteous and disciplined, although enriched and enlivened by the Chinese traditions and philosophy which became the subject of my scholar-father's lifelong study.

Therefore I feel at home in Philadelphia. I like the atmosphere of age, the air of a deserved self-confidence, the presence of fine music and art. Of all American cities I consider it the most cultivated.

TFH: My work piled up. My secretary, good though she is, simply could not keep up with everything. We had become particularly attached to one of the young maids at the hotel because of the way she worked. We began to employ her for a couple of hours after work each day to help with the filing. God, how I worried about money! I was right about the response of the American people. They wrote letters saying they were glad we were doing something. They asked ways in which they could help. They offered to bake cookies and knit sweaters, they prayed. They did everything but send money! Expenses mounted. I knew that you would give everything you had if necessary to get this thing started. You told me, in fact, that you intended to pay all administrative costs yourself for as long as you could so that any money given us could go directly to the children. How far could this go? I had no wish to have the Foundation become a burden to you. I wanted it to be a joy. Fret! Fret! Worry!

For at least an hour each day I looked at houses. Some of the places I saw you wouldn't believe existed and the moment anyone found out for whom I was looking, up went the price. It's a shame that some of the people in business in our country seem to feel it's all right to charge what the traffic will bear. How many times in the past months have I heard it said, "She's got it! Let her spend it!"

I've grown to resent that. I've built up a pure hatred for this attitude which has since caused me to order people out of my office, indeed out of my sight, the moment I get wind of it. People who try this sort of thing are trying to take the food away from hungry children we are trying so desperately to care for.

About this time a new realtor came into my life, one of the younger members of an old-established, reputable real estate firm in Philadelphia, still manned by the family who founded it. He saw at once my problem and said:

"Let me see if I can find the place for you."

I can tell you I was glad to let him try. Time passed slowly until he called and told me he had two for me to see. Armed with my determination to have only the right one, I ventured forth to look again. Bitter, bitter disappointment! They were nice but they were just houses, nothing special, nothing distinctive to separate them from the hundreds of other houses. In my despair I turned to him on that afternoon, early in May, and said:

"Please, isn't there any house in Philadelphia that will do?"

He then said:

"Well, there is one but it's expensive. That is why I didn't show it to you."

My heart fell at the word expensive, but I asked to see it anyway. We then walked to 2019 Delancey Place. From the appearance of the building, the street it was on, I knew at once that I had found our home, although I didn't know how we would ever get it. I walked through its wide elegant halls, mounted the curving staircase, and I knew you had to see it that very afternoon.

PSB: I remember—I remember! Houses are important because they are places for people. I do not believe in luxury for luxury's sake—that is extravagance. But beauty is essential for people who love beauty. I am not one of those persons who can work anywhere. In distasteful surroundings I simply do not work. If I force myself, the result is worthless. Creative work comes from the inner spirit and if the spirit is annoyed, irritated, dismayed, it does not produce its best. A vase of half-dead flowers on my desk, for example, can cost me a thousand dollars of good work. It is cheaper for me to get fresh flowers.

In the same way on a greater scale I knew that it would be too expensive for me—and for you—to go into the unattractive quarters. We could not do our best work here. And the task we have set ourselves to is so far-reaching and so important that unless we do our best all will be waste.

There is another reason, too, why I wanted the house to be beautiful—"elegant but not extravagant," as someone has described it. During my long career there is an accumulation of objects that I treasure, various gifts and awards that until now have been put away. I wanted to share them with people. Our family house, overflowing with guests and children, has not been a suitable place for them. Now it occurred to me that the house in Philadelphia would serve to house them and let them be shown to my readers, those who, in a sense, had made it possible for me to receive such awards. I proposed that when the house was finished it be put on exhibition and the money thus earned be added to the fund for the children who are lost unless they are found. This is how it happens that the Chinese things I own are now in that house, the prizes and awards, the family Bible, the paintings, ancient Chinese faces, art objects, and manuscripts, the leather-bound first editions of my books. I feel content to know that in this way, too, my life is of use and will so continue to be when I am no longer here in this body that now contains me.

The house, as our headquarters, must be one we two could

enjoy. It must suit the work we have to do and yet beauty must be in its atmosphere. I knew the moment I entered that house it was the right one. It is not very large, only two rooms to a floor, with the wide halls. The décor, as I first saw it, was of course impossible for us. What suits one person is seldom what suits another. But the house itself is beautiful in its simplicity and its lines. I could see all the garish green and gold taken away and replaced by cool pastel shades, with plenty of white. It is a French house, more than a century old, designed for a French lady by a man who loved her and made her his wife. Someone else did the green and gold. It was wrong and I wanted it gone, immediately.

Now it is gone. Soon the house will be itself again, the arches restored to the halls between drawing room and dining room—that was your brilliant idea—and the offices on the first floor in full use. We have grown too fast, of course. Already we are planning more work space—indeed we must have it. But the house at 2019 Delancey Place will continue to be the heart of our work.

It was you, however, who thought of using my personal seal on the door, my name in ancient Chinese script carved upon jade, as the mark of the Foundation. It has stood upon my desk for decades, of no use to anyone except to me. Now I am proud that it will be used for the benefit of thousands of children who belong both to America and Asia. Yes, that was a happy day when I first walked into the house.

TFH: Whoa! You are going much too fast! It was far from that easy!

After we had seen the house I think we both knew that no other would ever do, but we hemmed and hedged with each other. I know I was hesitant to suggest we spend that much of your money. I think you hesitated to make the decision because I was the one to live there. So we waited, I holding my breath and you taking the firm stand that you would not be the one to decide. Two weeks passed before the realtor called and told me that someone else was making an offer for the house. I called you at once from the Drake. By now our office there was completely overrun with mail, printers and salesmen constantly giving me no chance to think, let alone carry on a coherent conversation on the phone.

"Really," you said, "do you think you could be happy living in that house? I know it would be good for our offices but you will be living there!"

"Well, yes," I ventured, "I can be happy living anywhere. It's just that it's so much money!"

At that you said, "Well, I don't think we should let this house get away. We must have the right place and I'll get the money from somewhere. You must tell them at once that we will take it."

TFH: Tell them at once I did! It was when the papers were all ready to sign and I was sitting in our attorney's office that we discovered the problem with zoning. The house was not zoned for our sort of business and furthermore we were told it was impossible for it to be so zoned.

"The twenty hundred block of Delancey Place," they said, "is the finest residential section of Center City Philadelphia. It has been preserved as such for many years. The residents of the block will never allow it to be zoned for offices."

Problems! Problems! Bitter disappointment again!

Of course I called you and reported my findings.

"But we must have that house," you said in consternation, "why can't it be zoned?"

Try though I did to explain all the reasons they gave, your observation was:

"But those are exactly the reasons we must have that house. When we get on that block we will fight harder than anyone else to keep it from being commercial. Our offices cannot be next to a gas station or a barber shop. We must try."

I passed on your decision to the attorneys and much to their distaste they allowed us to sign a conditional agreement of sale based on whether zoning could be had. Nothing to do now but wait! They told us it would take about thirty days before we would know.

In the meantime, business had to go on. We scheduled a visit to Washington in order to visit the State Department and the Defense Department and let them know what we were up to. The State Department promised to help us in every way they could unofficially, the Defense Department was kind and interested, said they didn't think they could help but would try. We decided also to talk the whole thing over with Robert Kennedy, then Attorney General of the United States, and ask his help as a member of our Board of Governors. I'll never forget my first sight of him that day in May, a little man with burning eyes, a great man, nevertheless, and destined to be greater, I believe, sitting behind that enormous desk, with a striking resemblance to his brother. We had visited Sargent Shriver earlier and he had agreed, too, to serve on our Board of Governors, and it was this important victory I think that gave us courage to go after the Attorney General.

PSB: I am one of the millions everywhere in the world who will never recover from the death of John Fitzgerald Kennedy and the way it came about. I love my country, I am proud to be American but not as proud as I was before. Such things can happen here! I should have been prepared for it by other cruel deaths which had gone before, by the lawlessness of lynchings, by murders not prosecuted, by murderers unpunished. All such acts led to the murder of John F. Kennedy, President of the United States of America. Lawlessness runs like an evil stream in our blood. There are still those who think themselves beyond and above the law, those who take up a gun to avenge and consider it a right. These are the unAmericans, these are the ones who destroy the fabric of law and order which we call civilization and which is our only protection. In every lawless act we are all jeopardized. These are the criminals.

Ah, but I was proud to be an American that night when face to face I first saw President Kennedy and his wife Jacqueline! We were waiting in the East Room of the White House, we Nobel Prize winners. It was the occasion of a dinner given in our honor. We had been talking together for half an hour and more, but in reality we were waiting for the President. Nothing else at that moment was important. Suddenly we heard music. We turned to the wide-flung doors and saw the glittering guardsmen marching in carrying flags. Behind them were the two handsomest people in the world, young, beautiful, brilliant, successful. We burst into applause, every one of us so proud that we were between tears and smiles. They made the evening for us. The dinner was not exceptional as to food, the entertainment rather dull in spite of Fredric March as the interlocutor, but because of the royal young couple, the night shone as day.

Since then all that has happened has enshrined both of them permanently, the one dead, the other still living, and with them their children. The password is beauty, in the full meaning of the word. In recent years we have all in many ways been robbed of beauty, but they restored it to us for a time, these two. I would say that it has perished from the face of the earth save that beauty is imperishable.

This beauty has touched every member of the Kennedy family. I felt it when we visited Sargent Shriver, surely one of the great good men of our time. I knew it when we sat in front of Robert Kennedy's big desk. He looked at us across its vast expanse and at first I thought him remote and cold. He said what we expected, that it would not be possible for him to—

I stopped him, do you remember? I simply could not let him say no. I kept talk going. I brought the children to him. I told him how much they needed a man whom all the world knew and trusted, not only for what he himself had done, but because of the President, now dead.

He listened, his eyes burning on me, a resolute strong face so like his brother's, as you say, yet individual in its difference. I did my best and waited. Suddenly he rose to his feet. He was taller than I thought. He put out his hand.

"You may use my name," he said, and his handshake was firm.

TFH: Our Board of Governors grew more impressive by the hour. Now of course the list includes the great from every part of our country. The lost children need such people to give them a status, for they have no status of their own. It is my hope and belief, too, that the peoples in Asian countries where our American servicemen are stationed will read these names and conclude that these children, hitherto unwanted, are wanted after all, and by important persons. Our offices at the Drake grew steadily more confusing and crowded. By now Jimmy had left his camera store work and come with us full time to help with the mailings and other general office work, but mainly to be our own photographer on our first Korean trip. We then planned to go in the late fall of 1964. My assistant while I was still at the studio had left there and was trying to decide what type of job he wanted. I asked him to come to work with us and take over arrangements for the benefit balls already being planned in many cities. I had also managed to convince you that we should make a small appeal for funds via direct mail at Christmas in order to test it and see if we could raise funds in this way. We had started doing business with an up-and-coming young printer in Philadelphia with his own business. I discovered that he is actually much more than a printer. He is a direct mail expert and I'm sure he thought me mad as I talked of all the things we were going to do. But I had watched how you never let anything stop you, so I carried on, not always calmly, I'll admit! When I became discouraged I reminded myself that all of your friends and even the agent to whom you first submitted your work had told you that you should stop writing because no one was interested in stories about China. It was miserably hot that May and there was no air conditioning in our small office so you were apt to find me working barefooted and in Bermuda shorts. I made a pest of myself by calling our attorney many times a day, to see if they had heard anything about the house. No word! No word! I pity those who must wait!

You really kept me going those days, singlehandedly, telling me of your amazing life, and of all the things you had done. I'll never understand why we talk the way we do, for I know I've told you things I've never told anyone and I'm sure you have done the same with me. It was during such a talk that you told me of Richard J. Walsh, your amazing court-ship that spanned continents, and parts of your twenty-five years together right down to the end of his life and his beautiful last words.

PSB: I can look back on my marriage now and see it as it was. During the days when he was here, I only knew I was happy. Today, upon your question, I ask myself why I was happy, and of what that happiness consisted. I think it was freedom. He loved me as I was, and I knew it. I knew he did not want me changed, saw no reason for changing me, willful ways and all. Therefore I lived in freedom. I had nothing to hide. I was never afraid to speak, to act, to come, to go, to withdraw into solitude if I wished, and sometimes I do wish. Nor did it occur to me to want him changed. I loved him, so why try to change him? We enjoyed each other's company, preferred not to be separated, and declined any occasion that might separate us. Did we never argue? Of course we did, for we had independent minds and it was interesting to argue. Sometimes one even convinced the other.

Only one subject did we finally decide one day never to argue again. It was the subject of life after death. He was a convinced atheist and believed that all life ended with death. My position was, it seemed to me, more scientific. It was simply that one cannot decide without facts, and so far what happens after death is only in the area of faith and hypothesis. Then, too, neither of us could bear to think of the death of the other. It was insupportable and we simply could not consider it. I am glad that he never knew he was dying, his brilliant brain fading slowly into unawareness of everything and everyone. When the last moment came it was in his sleep. But of this I have written in *A Bridge for Passing*.

I think, however, that he knew that the time was coming when he would not be able to communicate, for he thought of one thing and another that he wanted to say while he could still speak. It was on one such day, before the light went out in him, but near the end, so that it was the very last of the lovely things he said, that he turned his head to hear my footsteps. His eyesight was destroyed. When I came to his bedside, he took my hand and said slowly but quite clearly, although words were already difficult for him:

"Thank you—for infinite variety."

What he thanked me for was something he himself made possible. By his approving love he gave me the freedom to be myself.

II

TFH: You and I talked much about the half-American children and their tragic way of life and what we would do to change matters. We have agreed now that this is the problem of the American people and that it's through the generosity of John Q. Average Public that the major portion of our funds will come. We have had the heartbreaking experience of meeting with people who could easily give us a million dollars and save more than that in taxes, only to have them say:

"You are doing a wonderful work. It's a much needed and worthwhile project but I can't help you."

The letter I cherish most in the Foundation reads:

"My tiny contribution represents many small self-denials. . . ."

This kind lady sent four dollars.

Or the high school girl in California who wrote:

"I have been saving my allowance for two years now to help with expenses when I go to college. I don't need the extras as much as these poor ones need necessities."

She sent sixty dollars and has since organized a committee of her teen-age friends to raise funds for these children!

Yet, believe it or not, one of the richest and best-known ladies in our land just sent us five dollars! We appreciate all the help we can get but the contrast between the generosity of "John Q" and the very rich is marked in favor of "John Q." We intend to make it known all over the world that our Foundation is not the well-known "tax dodge" of the wealthy but the way for the American public to help their grandsons, sons, half sisters and brothers who are outcasts, starving in the lands of their births *because* they are half-American. The Foundation is merely acting as "Guardian" representing the American half of the child's heritage. As I sit here at the table in your Vermont home, nestled into the side of a mountain near Manchester, I am moved immeasurably when I remember the Social Security retirement check for $12.76 which an old gentleman in California has been sending every month for the past four months. There is never a note or a word, just the check, but with that gesture the story of a life is told.

Our responsibility to the American people is overwhelming. We have been advised that we must earmark a percentage of each contribution to cover the cost of administration, and we have insisted that it be held down to twenty-five percent, which is far below the national average if I'm to believe what we have been told. But the mere thought of withholding even twenty-five percent of that Social Security check completely destroys any vestige of self-respect I might have gathered. I know you feel the same way, for we have discussed many times the possibility of finding other ways to meet the administrative costs of our project. The royalties on this book provide one of these ways and there will be others.

Another thing that makes us both feel better, I'm sure, is that without administration, the children get nothing. This brings to mind the story of the ex-serviceman who married his Korean girl when he found she was to bear his child. They were divorced after the birth, and he has since acquired an American wife, but he has been sending over eleven hundred dollars per year to support his child in Korea. We have had to tell him that, in your opinion, someone is taking great advantage of him, for that amount of money could support an entire village there. This gives another important need for our service. American money must be represented in these lands, desperately poor, but we must be sure it is used for the purposes intended. It is common knowledge that American money has been misused in many instances abroad and has purchased for us only hatred instead of the friendship that everyone knows cannot be bought. A recent letter from a Korean friend describes some of the various "Christian" movements in that country. I question whether they are truly as "Christian" as Christ intended, but at any rate he says that these so-called Christian missionaries do a great deal of good but then destroy all feeling of gratitude and love by insisting that those helped, perfectly happy and religious in their way, follow the faith of the helper. How un-American can one get? And what kind of picture is this to present to other lands of our country? Supposedly our country was founded to give freedom of worship. What then are we doing? Here is the letter:

"During and after the Korean War, there were many foreign voluntary agencies—most of them being American— helping orphans and others. Most agencies now are supported by religious groups in their home countries, and have been helping those people in their respective religions. Were there so many religious groups and their members in Korea? Well, you've got to be a member, if you want the donation of that agency. Thus, much money is spent for social welfare, but with strings attached thereto. And, although I hate to admit it, it is true that many Koreans have reluctantly become Christians because of these strings.

"I remember I read an article, 'Why are we Americans hated by Asians?' which appeared in a magazine published in Japan, I think, about four or so years ago. I am in no position to say anything about Vietnam. But are Frenchmen welcome in Vietnam, where French-evangelized Catholics and Buddhists are fighting each other so fiercely? What about Americans there? Is there any correlation between the attitude of Buddhists in Vietnam toward Frenchmen and the same toward their fellow Catholics?

"Here in Korea, there is a stronger antagonism between Christian denominations than betweeen Christians and heathens! After the Korean War broke out in 1950, more and more missionaries were sent to Korea from America mainly, and they established, with the help of the above-mentioned agencies, a number of new denominations, each of which has been overemphasizing its own doctrines. The results are decorated by statistics of an ever increasing membership. The agencies are here to help improve the economic status of the poorer in Korea. They might have been successful, but in their attempt they have also increased the number of religious strata of the Korean society. When Christian denominations are struggling, one against another, or calling each other names, the non-Christian Korean will of course denounce

Korean Christians, but they will also say, 'See what Americans, or their missionaries, or their dollars left behind.'

"It is paradoxical again that money is here to help 'integrate' the racially mixed children, but is also being used to 'segregate' them into religious sects. Although I belong to a Christian church myself, I stand against this policy. It does not matter where money comes from, or who donates. The donator just should not force the recipients to follow his faith. I have just outlined my views as a Korean. Now, you may well ask for opinions of an American in Korea."

Really, I think this is shocking but how many times have you told me that Asians say:

"Missionaries, traders, and armies come together!"

God knows how many half-American children are in Japan, Okinawa and now cropping up in Vietnam and elsewhere with no end in sight! I knew you could not afford to support this work alone. You seemed to feel that we should go to a few individuals who have access to vast sums of money and ask their help. I didn't like to disagree with you then. I know now that if I do I should always speak and we will discuss a matter until we arrive on common ground. From past experience I knew that the hardest people to get money from are those who have it. After all, that's why they have it. Moreover, I felt that this problem belongs to the American people. These men who go abroad and father these children are not strangers to us. They are raised in our homes. They go to our schools and churches. American society is at least partly responsible for their conduct. It has been my experience that the American people are willing to accept their responsibility if they are made aware of it. I knew that if we were going to ask a few people for a lot of money it would take time. I also knew we needed help at once. But where was it to come from? Remember the woman, rich and famous, who gave us five dollars?

PSB: We are learning a great deal about people, you and I. Yes, the disappointments are in the ones who could give and should, for wealth brings responsibility. I confess that five dollars from one of the richest and best-known women in our country, the wife of a famous military man to boot, who herself must have seen the children for whom we work, made me very angry. I wish she had sent us nothing, for then we might have thought she had not received our letter of appeal. But five dollars from a millionaire shows only contempt for the children. I do not forgive her. And though I share your affection for those who cannot afford to give and yet do give, it is not fair that they assume the whole burden of our responsibility for the half-American children.

We have the responsibility, too, as you say, for seeing that American money is spent in other countries for the purposes for which it is given. I have lived too long in countries so poor that dishonesty was almost a way of life. It is inevitable that trickery, lies, theft, become habitual in such places, not only of necessity, but as signs of rebellion against hated rulers.

Then there are these countries which are struggling to establish governments of their own, after years of foreign rule, such countries as India, Korea, Vietnam. When the foreign governments depart, the new young national governments are insecure and corruption becomes a safeguard. Officials, knowing they may lose their posts at any moment, accumulate secret hoards.

It is not quite honest, and yet it is not quite theft. Somehow, Christian and non-Christian, we must work for the welfare of the children who belong to us all.

TFH: The date of our appearance before the zoning board was set finally for June. Oh, what a dreadful wait it was! By now there were four of us working in that small office at the Drake and concentrated thought on any subject was scarcely possible. Yet it was necessary to get a zoning variance for our building.

PSB: And I was new to the ways of American cities! I had heard of zoning, of course, but had never been concerned with it in my farmhouse home. Now for the sake of the children, I met with the dwellers on our street and tried to explain why we wanted to be there. We found them kind, you remember, if not altogether comprehending, as yet, and finally they were willing for us to buy the house once they were assured that it was not for commercial purposes.

Still there was the zoning board to face!

It was a desperately hot day, I remember. I put on a thin black suit with a wide white collar and wore a big white hat. Odd you haven't mentioned my hats yet! And as usual I took a fan with me, a habit acquired years ago in Asia. I was thankful for it, too, for the air in the board room was hot, and there were many formidable-looking people there. I was not really nervous, in spite of all that. I am afraid I am used to having my own way.

TFH: Mention your hats? Yes I will, though I could write a book about them alone. You wear them big because, you say:

"I can hide under them and no one will know it is I."

My dear, I hate to disillusion you but it has come to the point that whenever someone sees a big hat on the street or in a restaurant in Philadelphia he or she says:

"There, isn't that Pearl Buck?"

As to your being used to getting your own way, the one light touch of that zoning board appearance was my overhearing a conversation in the hall afterwards. An attorney representing one of the citizens' groups said to one of the leading citizens on our block:

"One thing you can bet on. If she wants it, she will get it, she has more pull than God!"

I'm afraid I laughed out loud right there, as did you when I repeated it to you later.

"Pull" you have, yes! You always go straight to the top. But I have never known you to use your influence for yourself, your own family—or anyone else as a matter of fact, except when it is necessary for these children for whom we work.

It seems to me that you treat people's respect for you as a sacred trust and something which you must strive to live up to.

PSB: The real reason I wear big hats is because I look silly in little ones, and it is true that I make it a point of personal honor never to use special influence for myself or my family. And I value the trust that people have in me. In a sense, no private life is possible after the public creates its own image of one. I sometimes feel it necessary to apologize to my own children for being their mother, for they suffer from my public image and cannot commit the usual small sins of youth without news of it being brought to me. They marvel at my acumen.

"How did you know!" they cry.

Well, there is always someone who tells what so-and-so said another so-and-so saw my child do.

"Why are you in the encyclopedia?" an eleven-year-old son demanded of me one day.

I felt too shy to explain. Let him find out for himself, if he must!

"Funny, isn't it?" I murmured.

But the public image prevails. There are places I cannot go and things I must not do, and these extend to my children, too.

I heard one daughter whisper to another. "It doesn't matter what they do—they're nobody so they can do what they like. I wish we could!"

Is this good, this public image? I am used to it, was used to it even in the China I knew, for there it was the responsibility of every member, young and old, in every family, but especially in a proud American family like ours, to maintain its public image in the community. *Noblesse oblige?* I believe in it!

TFH: Finally the zoning permit came through. Of course our staff tried to convince me not to move into the new house until it had been cleaned and painted. They reminded me of the horrible green and gold paint and the three-years accumulation of dust and dirt natural in a house that has stood empty for so long. But I picked up my dictaphone again and moved that very day, and no matter how much they all objected our staff went with me. On Monday we opened up as usual except that now we were in our new home, where we had every intention of staying for the next century at least. Of course everything was complete confusion that Monday. In the first place, as everyone in business knows, Mondays are always confusion, with the desperate efforts to locate files and folders, correspondence, pens, typewriters, etc., etc. Somehow we managed to get through that day. I remember I left my desk long after midnight and went upstairs to my bedroom on the fourth floor and slept on a couch pillow on the floor. I refused to return to the apartment at the hotel. What a night! Sleeping on the floor in a huge empty house is not exactly my cup of tea, but that time I was indescribably happy doing it.

I awoke the next morning with a start and stared around at a huge empty room. I was not able to remember at first where I was or how I got there. Recollection came fast, however, as the moving men began to bring in the furniture promptly at 8:30. We were off to another day. You came in around noon as we were having luncheon with someone or other, and I'll never forget the look on your face as you looked around at the green and gold and said:

"Oh dear, I hope we haven't done the wrong thing!"

PSB: You are a determined character and that is the reason I chose you for the job. We complement each other in excellent fashion. You with your redhead temper lose patience and immediately fly into your "highly irritated" state. It is extremely effective and produces startling results in your vicinity. That day in your crowded hotel apartment I saw, the moment I walked in, was such a crisis. Electric sparks surrounded you—sparks of frustration. You were doing a big job in a small place—too small. It was time to act. I did so. When I found that the delay was the fault of our own legal firm—excellent though they are and they with eighty lawyers!—I was suddenly and finally angry. Yes, it is true I will not use influence for personal reasons. But behind all we do now I see thousands of piteous children, waiting.

Your anger is swift and hot. Mine is slow to come but deadly cold. My long Asian training has something to do, perhaps, with both slowness and chill. I do not like to be angry. It consumes energy that I prefer to use in other ways. Moreover, I was taught by my old Confucian tutor in my childhood that the superior person does not show anger, even if he feels it. Of course I know that this philosophy has nothing to do with you, for you are American. But mind and soul, I was trained in Asia and something clings.

As for my expression when I walked into the house the next day—well, it was all that green and gold. It made me feel liverish. But the feeling I had was familiar. Checking my memory, I realized that once before I had walked into a house and felt the same revulsion. It was in China, on a cold March day, the year 1927, when the Communist armies took the city of Nanking where I was living. Mobs of rowdies came with them to plunder the houses where white people had lived. My house was so wrecked. I did not see it for nearly two years, during which time it had been used as a base for cholera-stricken Communist soldiers and was in a state of filth and confusion when I returned. It was after the Nationalists had driven the Communist armies away. Where to begin the restoration!

The same despair fell upon me that day as I surveyed the vistas of worn green and gold. Where to begin! But you of course had already begun. You had ordered gallons of off-white paint and someone was painting.

TFH: The tour plans were shaping up quite well by then, and the man in charge of that department in the Foundation was busy from morning until night getting out letters to various cities, telling them about the wonderful help they were giving the children through their benefit balls. The response was mixed with wonder and disbelief that Pearl S. Buck was actually coming to town and was coming to attend a ball! That proves my point, my dear. As I've said from the beginning, your public really doesn't know you. They love the sketchy picture they have of you from your various books, but they would love the real complete you much more if they only had the chance. You, with your shy retiring ways and rather sheltered life, are depriving the American people of something they richly deserve. You haven't given them a chance to know you as you are, gay, fun-loving, smoking a small cigar if you feel like it, dancing long past midnight because you love it, yet poised, beautiful and gracious, always a great lady because you wouldn't know how to be different. How many times you have said to me:

"People aren't really interested in me, they just like my books!"

Well, you are wrong, my dear! I'm sure that people like your books because they are you. You, least of all, have understood your success. It's people, and their love for that which is great. I use as an example excerpts from two lectures given at Stockholm University, Sweden, by a man who once had a strong prejudice against China, women writers and against you. This, my dear, is the power of your love for people. He says:

"I find myself in the embarrassing position of being singularly unqualified to criticize the works of Pearl Buck. To me she is the most nearly perfect writer America has produced in this century. She is surely the most articulate and she exercises complete control over the tools of her trade. She writes perfect (and perfectly readable) sentences and absolutely logical and graceful paragraphs and builds these into clearly defined chapters or sections. She understands exactly and without any hedging what constitutes a novel and what distinguishes it from a short story. She creates a group of interesting characters, makes certain that at least one of these is one with whom the reader will at once identify himself. Then she proceeds to set this character up in conflict with society and sees to it that the character either defeats society or the other way around. And she does not forget for a single instant that all of this (as necessary as it is) is to no avail if the entire structure does not rest unshiftingly on a valid premise. It is Pearl Buck's conscientious attention to premise that makes her not just an excellent writer but a great one.

"The only possible thing I can find in Pearl Buck to annoy me (no, irritate is a better word) is that she makes the whole thing look too easy. And I am convinced that for her it isn't as difficult as it is for the rest of us. I loathe writing. It is the most awful and most demanding and most exhausting work I have ever performed. When the fit is on me and I am in the terrible throes of creating a piece of writing, I often think that I'd far rather undergo an anestheticless appendectomy by flickering candlelight with a rusty scissors on a kitchen table in a jungle tent during a blowing rainstorm with wild animals shrieking complaint than to ever have to write something again. Pearl Buck, so I am told, can spend the morning hoeing or separating and setting out beds of Shasta daisies or putting up preserves or tending a case of pink eye or vacuuming a thousand carpets and then sit down calmly at once in the afternoon and turn her mind away from everything except what it is that she has set herself down to do and write. 'Why not?' she says. 'I am a writer.'

"I long to write a biography of Pearl Buck but I am afraid to do so, afraid that I won't be able to see the warts (and so far I have not been able to detect a single one); and I am frightened, too, that I would never be able to do justice to her. I sometimes wake in the night after having dreamed that I have been asked to paint a portrait of El Greco or to design a suit for Chanel or teach Gertrude Ederle the Australian crawl or some such unlikely thing and I am so undone (because, of course, in the nightmare I always agree with alacrity to do whatever it is) that further sleep is impossible and so I have to get up (as my mother says) and 'put on the oatmeal' for breakfast. It's much the same way with the biography I want to do of Pearl Buck. It must be done but I don't know if I am the man to do it.

"Pearl Buck displays in *East Wind: West Wind* and *The Good Earth* two of her many styles. She has at least five or six. She has the scholarly, dignified Chinese style and the rough peasant Chinese style which these illustrate. In addition she has her American style, her essay and lecture style, and her children's style, for she has written charming stories for the very young. And perhaps she has what might be described as her John Sedges style. I am not sure about this last inasmuch as I have not read her 'John Sedges' novels. But it stands to reason that she wouldn't have risked publishing under a pseudonym anything that was recognizably Pearl Buck. No matter which style Pearl Buck employs, her instrument is always tuned to concert pitch and she is able to transpose and improvise with the greatest of ease. And through all the styles runs the inevitable bright thread of freedom.

"Now, there exist a vast number of subjects which I find that I am unable to read about, at least to the extent that I cannot devote to them the attention they deserve. The list is long and varied and it includes: Jewish family life (which is always described in terms so cloying and gagging); the Irish Civil War; the Welsh mining problem (Richard Llewellyn to the contrary); anything which involves someone disguising himself as someone else and fooling no one but the author; and a dozen others. It's not that I'm prejudiced. To the contrary, I am rather like the woman who said she *hated* prejudice. I deplore it. There is a blindness about it unworthy of human effort. One must learn tolerance. I have, to my profound sorrow, two prejudices. One concerns a certain religious persuasion (not Catholic; not Jewish), and one concerns something entirely different. I am proud of neither. I am so distressed by both that I have attempted these past three years to rid myself entirely of the latter (with some small degree of success) and to temper, at least, my feelings about the former to the extent that I can think of it without wanting to call the police. But: books about some things I am constitutionally unable to read. This is all by way of easing you into the terrible knowledge that until I undertook the research for these lectures, I simply could not make myself read anything about China or the Chinese. You will, perhaps, be astonished to learn that I had never read anything that Pearl Buck had ever written. I already knew that I wouldn't like her. I already knew that the Chinese were of no interest to me whatever. It was not that I thought she was a writer without merit. It was merely that, regrettably, she had chosen a subject which lay far outside my field of interest. Imagine my surprise, then, when I had to read her, I couldn't put her down. I have read four or five of her books at least four or five times each. She has made China and the Chinese interesting for me. They have come alive through her genius. She has made me ashamed that I have neglected them for so long. I can offer her no greater personal compliment than this. And I can see quite clearly that all that is keeping me away from the other subjects on my list is lack of a competent spokesman.

"Now and again a book comes out which has the appearance of a minor classic from the day of publication. So it was with *The Good Earth*. The critical acclaim that welcomed it, the spectacularly increasing sales, and the universal recognition of its excellence have secured and fixed this initial impression. It has become a matter of record. It is a classic. It is a sound, literate treatment of what, until that hour of its publication, was an almost unknown subject. It is still, nearly thirty years later, the best available guide to peasant China and its problems.

"For three decades now (although she has carefully ignored it and pushed ever on into the blazing noon of other subjects) Pearl Buck has lived in the shadow of *The Good Earth*'s unique excellencies. It is good for her career that the muted *East Wind: West Wind* appeared before *The Good Earth*. If it had been the other way around, it might have been disastrous. *The Good Earth* was so vigorous that *East Wind: West Wind* would never have received the attention it deserved, and the critics would have wondered what had happened to Pearl Buck's talent which had promised so much (too much, in a first work) in *The Good Earth*. Pearl Buck's career would have been a long time recovering from the resulting shock. (I once saw Judith Anderson in *Medea*. The very instant she opened her mouth for the first time, it was painfully obvious that she had begun at a pitch she hadn't a prayer of being able to sustain, nor, worse, to top. So the whole play was done as one long scream which became less and less alarming.) Pearl Buck's career might never have been allowed the nuances of pitch which she has so beautifully displayed that she is capable of attaining, if she had begun with such a loud noise.

"Her other works appear not to be telling the same story but do not be deceived: they are. For Pearl Buck there is only one story: freedom. Freedom from every imaginable restriction that binds the spirit, the soul, the heart, the mind, the body of mankind. It is dressed up differently from time to time and set now in Japan, now in the United States, now somewhere else, and it is approached from another angle, but the subject is always the same. It is a tribute to Pearl Buck's skill as a writer that she manages each time around to make it all seem fresh and new and more suddenly urgent than ever before. It cannot be said of her (as it can be, for example, of William Faulkner) that her work is rich in contradiction. It is straightforward, one-tracked, single-purposed. Pearl Buck is the least ambiguous of any major contemporary writer. Anybody on earth can read and understand Pearl Buck. Practically everybody on earth does. She is the most widely translated of any modern writer in the English language. In pursuit of her villain, Pearl Buck has produced some of the most acutely relevant writing anyone now alive is ever likely to be privileged to read. The breadth of her insight into the current and eternal problems that all mankind is almost beyond measure. The problems she proposes do not perplex her. She knows how they can be solved. She comes face to face with them and stares them down. Her perceptions have extraordinary solidity.

"Pearl Buck has no love for odd and unusual words and she

is not an experimenter, in the ordinarily understood sense, with rhythms of speech. Examples of what might be thought to be this (I am thinking especially of *East Wind: West Wind*) are not deliberate experiments. The beautiful cadences of *East Wind: West Wind* are the direct result of Pearl Buck's having *written* in English while *thinking* in *Chinese*. The poetry of her prose in this and comparable works is the natural result of such mental gymnastics, not the consequence of having sat down and said 'Now let me see if I can't find a way to make my characters sound Chinese.' The gallimaufry that comes from that kind of experimenting is altogether too evident in the pidgin English resorted to by the hundreds of hack writers who have had the effrontery to challenge Pearl Buck on her home ground. Pearl Buck believes that the purpose of language is communication, not deliberate obscurity. Language is Pearl Buck's oyster. Her efforts in behalf of communication have caused certain undiscerning critics to describe her as a simple writer. Nothing could be wider of the mark. Distinguished, non-patronizing simplicity of style is very hard to come by. Pearl Buck's several styles are all so deceptively simple that they constitute a snare by which more than one imitator has been caught.

"What is so fine about Pearl Buck is that she never seeks to minimize or obscure the problems she so passionately pictures. She dissects and illuminates, fearlessly, everything she recognizes as evil and she issues no namby-pamby bulletins raising false hopes. She says here it is and it's terrible and something has got to be done about it or it's going to get worse. But she is no Schopenhauer nor even a Franz Kafka. Hope abounds in her pages. It casts an always brave, sometimes feeble, sometimes blazing, light on even the most forlorn and dismal of her realities. Pearl Buck's version of someone's brilliant observation that power corrupts and absolute power corrupts absolutely is: love conquers and complete love conquers completely. She emphatically denies the currently fashionable notion that although all men are equal some are more equal than others.

"Phoney critics never tire of saying that *The Good Earth* is the only book Pearl Buck has ever written. I am driven to the conclusion that they have not troubled to read her great American novel, *The Townsman*, nor her latest book, *The Living Reed*. It's easy enough to make a snide remark but it's awfully hard to make it stick if it has no basis in fact. American critics are (for reasons I have never been able to fathom) bitterly jealous of Pearl Buck's success. It may be that they think she is Chinese, although what this would have to do with it, I cannot suggest. They don't know what to do with her. They would like to erase her name from the list of American writers and give her to the Asians (who, oddly, already claim her). But those critics who deny her Americanism have never heard her lecture nor read one of her essays nor troubled at all to read beyond *The Good Earth*. Pearl Buck is fiercely and proudly American and Americans can be fiercely proud that she is one of them, that there is a member of the family ready, willing, and exquisitely capable of championing Americanism, of insuring that it counts for something in the day-to-day and eternity-to-eternity business of world relations."*

PSB: I perceive your tactics. By all kinds of flattery you

* From a course on the six U.S. winners of the Nobel Literature prize currently given by Jason Lindsey at the Kursverksamheten of Stockholm University. Quoted by permission of the author.

are determined to draw me out of this comfortable shell in which I seek shelter. Yes, I know Jason Lindsey has written me some charming letters, but we've never met. Don't ask me why I am shy! Don't say it is ridiculous because I know it is. Am I to blame China for it? Perhaps, and on double account. First, as I have said, I was a white child living among brown people and however friendly they were, and they were, I was aware of my difference. Second, I was trained by Asian women to be self-effacing. I do not regret this training, for it shaped me in profound and basic ways. I was taught the value and meaning of womanhood. I was taught how to behave with men, formally, informally and intimately, as occasion required, and this is precious knowledge. The Chinese women were old and wise and what they taught me has made it possible for me to enjoy my friendships with men, my working relationships with them, and my marriage. I have always been at ease in these relationships because I learned early the functions of being a woman. I have never competed with men in any area and have never felt the need to do so.

In honesty I am compelled to say, however, that I am not really as shy as I sometimes seem. It is partly training but training has become habit. Lin Yutang, the famous Chinese writer, was once visiting in my home and one day I felt his observant eyes upon me until finally I begged him to tell me why he kept watching me.

He took his pipe out of his mouth.

"You are Chinese," he said. "You move, speak and behave like a Chinese woman."

How could I help it? I was a woman long before I left China. Besides, I am not sure I want to be different. What I am has served me well enough. I have had and do have a happy life.

TFH: You have never had a public relations man or a press agent. You have always run from any form of publicity and here you dump the project of promoting the Foundation bearing your name into my lap! How far can I go? How much can I do? You said:

"I'll do anything I can for these children!"

Anything, eh? Fine, now what exactly did that mean?

"You go ahead and do what you think is right," you said, so I did! Press conferences, television and radio appearances, cocktail parties and luncheons, lectures and tours were arranged in the first twenty-one cities and I must say that with the exception of one city in Florida, we had wonderful cooperation from city officials, Chambers of Commerce, women's groups, schools, etc. In that one city, however, we were met with a blank impenetrable wall, perhaps because, as a city, they were having problems of their own at that time.

Our tour was scheduled to start on October ninth with the Pearl Buck Ball in Harrisburg, Pennsylvania. Everyone insisted that everything was scheduled at too fast and furious a pace for you. You, however, maintained that we were going on business and you wanted to be kept busy. I just ignored everyone and scheduled.

PSB: You are right. I like to be kept busy. I like traveling when it has a purpose, and we have a great purpose. Then, as you know, I am easily amused. I love sight-seeing when it can be included in our main program. I thoroughly enjoyed our few "get lost" days when we went to see the various sights, the underwater oceanic life centers, the fine old houses of the South, and an occasional art gallery or museum. But work was the order of our days and it was a delight to find that you work the way I do, without heed to time. Then, too, I like to dance and each ball was enjoyment, once the formalities were over. Cocktail parties I find less happy, for they are a succession of hands to be shaken and answers to be given to questions of little variety.

Then, too, there are the odd or perplexing situations. At one cocktail party, for example, a man greeted me warmly, and seated himself at my side on the couch.

"Tell me," he said. "Do you and your husband use thirty-thirty?"

I was puzzled but tried to reply. "I don't think so—but—"

He interrupted me. "I do! I'm a birdman myself."

He edged nearer, all enthusiasm, "You've done such wonderful things! Know what picture I like best? The one of you sitting on the elephant!"

Light broke. What should I do? Chinese training has taught me not to hurt anyone if it can be avoided. I did not want to hurt this kind man by telling him he had made a mistake and I was not Mrs. Frank Buck. I smiled and thanked him, others approached and he went away.

TFH: In the meantime, at the Foundation we were involved with many things. Your basic philosophy of "Do everything at once" was expressed at the start, so that is what we were doing. We felt we should not go into a big mailing without some knowledge of what our return would be so we were sending out one thousand letters of appeal per week to try to get some indication. Of course, again we were not prepared for the volume we were doing. This unpreparedness coupled with the natural difficulty of settling in a new building resulted in mass confusion. This confusion exceeded my wildest expectations as things progressed. We were faced, for example, with the problem of décor. Also, a very complicated telephone system had been installed. Our elevator had broken down and was keeping six repairmen busy. We were moving the kitchen out of the ground-floor work space and into the basement. Electricians worked on wiring and plumbers worked on the bathrooms upstairs, in need of repair after not being used for three years. One afternoon I stopped to think of all that was going on. There were ten telephone men, six elevator men, four plumbers, four electricians, three decorators measuring, a dozen or so volunteers folding and stuffing mail. My assistant and my secretary were discussing the Harrisburg ball schedule and helping with the mail. Jimmy was painting and giving directions to the various sets of workmen, while I, with my hunt and peck, relieved the typist on the autotype for lunch. Suddenly it struck me as funny. We had a good laugh, I took a walk, and it all started again.

PSB: You took a walk but you came back! I have the greatest sympathy with you when you want to escape. I practice escape habitually myself. Whatever work I am doing, it invariably tangles itself into a complexity, one potential leading into another, until the moment comes when I must escape all of it. Of course I come back. Work is interesting, if it is chosen work, and our work is both chosen and interesting. Why interesting? Because it is growing! Besides, you would not stay a moment if you did not love what you are doing—I know you! I know you have refused fabulous high-paying jobs because you did not find them interesting. All you want is enough money so you need not think about it, and can therefore wholeheartedly enjoy your work. That is what you have told me.

TFH: This same confusion has been going on ever since, believe me! Different sets of workers perhaps, but the same confusion! The returns from our direct mail were good enough so that we decided to go ahead and try 30,000 pieces for Christmas, as you know. We left everything and began the first of three tours across the country north and south, east and west.

I'll never forget the morning we left for Harrisburg, the first link of our journey. You had gone on ahead because you were taking your girls with you and they fill up your car. I was driving myself down and Jimmy was going along to take his pictures. We joined you at the hotel in Harrisburg and were off on our big adventure. I must say your friends there did a beautiful job. The ball was a great success, I'm sure you will agree. We stayed much later than we should have, for we both knew we had a ball the very next night in New Orleans. Nevertheless, as is characteristic of you, we stayed until almost the last dance before leaving for home to finish packing and catch a plane at 7:30 A.M. We met at the airport and as always you were right on time. I knew you had not slept but when I asked if you were tired you came on with your usual:

"No, I'm not tired! Do I look tired?"

I'll confess you didn't. But I wondered how you managed. I was exhausted! We boarded the plane and began to play Scrabble. Scrabble and chess seem to be the only two games you enjoy. I've never seen you play any other. Are these a carry-over from earlier years?

PSB: My mother enjoyed chess and taught me to play when I was very young. We played together until I went away to college, and never once in all those years did I win a game. I have often thought of her integrity in not letting me win. She was the better player and we both knew it, and she respected me too much to deceive me by giving me the game. I followed her example when I began to play chess with my own children. It was a real temptation when they were small and learning to play chess not to encourage them by allowing them to win sometimes, but remembering how I valued my mother's honesty, I gave my children the same respect. The time came when they could win honestly and then they properly appreciated what they achieved. This may seem unimportant, but I believe it is not. Children must be able to trust their parents in every incident and detail in mutual respect. A child never recovers, I believe, if he loses trust in a parent's honesty.

As for games, you know that I'm not good at them because, as I've told you, I have no sense of competition. Winning simply does not interest me. I enjoy chess and Scrabble because they engage my mind. Games of chance bore me and games of physical skill only a little less. You always win at Scrabble because you keep such a sharp eye on the figures, whereas I am only interested in making long complicated beautiful words regardless of my score. Each of us wins, I suppose, in his-her own way.

TFH: How could we possibly have known what the day in New Orleans would bring at that early stage of the game? Now, of course, after so many cities we would know better than to stay up all night before embarking to another city, but not then. After a press conference, three television tapings, a luncheon and a cocktail party, our hosts determined that our visit would not be complete without an evening on the town. It began with dinner at one of the fine old restaurants in the city. Then we were off to the hotel dance rooms for a night of gaiety. I watched as you danced joyously all evening and wondered how you managed to do it. With each passing moment I was growing less likely to make it back to the hotel, but you went on with your seemingly endless well of energy. Then the floor show started and as it droned on I watched you grow more bored. Actually the show was quite good, but I realized that evening that you are much the same as I am. If we want to see a show we go to a theater and when we want to dance we go to a night club or a ballroom, weary or not. That evening I made up my mind I would never see you that weary again. I learned then that I must be very firm when saying it's time to go home or you will always stay until the very last number is played and danced. You really must take good care of yourself and yet I know you are the last one to worry about yourself. I've wondered many times if, when you were a child, you got up and crept back downstairs to see what was going on after you were sent to bed. That devilish twinkle you get in your eyes sometimes leads me to believe that you were such a child.

PSB: It is true that as a child I roamed about in the night, if I woke, although a practical fear of the monstrous centipedes which walked in darkness made me carry a small oil lantern. These creatures abounded in the hot Chinese summer, especially in the rainy season, and they were fearsomely constructed. They were six to eight inches long, their segments were covered with hard black shell, each having a double pair of bright yellow legs, and on the tail a stinger, which could give a dangerous wound.

In spite of them I loved the soft tropical nights, the great luna moths, jade green and spotted with black and silver, clinging to the big gardenia bushes in the garden, and the bamboos, dim in the mists from the river. I wonder if my mother knew I wandered. If so, she said nothing then and never let me know afterwards.

TFH: The last number finally ended that night in New Orleans. I made our excuses and off we went back to our hotel amidst much grumbling from you about not being tired. I must say the ball was quite an affair. The money from that ball will feed a thousand children for one day in Korea. This knowledge made me know that we must go on and on as long as people are willing to raise money for us to carry on our work. And money it does take, my dear! Good intentions are all very wonderful but did you ever try them scrambled? Many people have good intentions and never accomplish anything. I am reminded of the would-be writers you tell about, and of the hours they spend talking of what they are going to write. Remember the man who has written you letters of twenty pages or more telling you all about the book he is going to begin, and asking your advice?

PSB: Yes, it is easy to make dream books. How many people write me long letters about them! The man you speak of—I need not tell his name. He writes so well, and describes in such careful detail his characters and plots that at first I was charmed into believing him a writer. But letter followed letter, each longer than the last, characters changed, plots developed, all in the letters, and at last I knew that there would never be a book. The man wrote himself out in letters.

For myself, I never write anything except the book itself. I forbid myself notes and outlines and all such approaches to the real job, which is to write a book. I do not let myself even talk about the book. My characters live only in my own mind until the moment comes when I introduce them on Page One and from then on they take over and the book is theirs.

TFH: I remember our conversation in the car as we drove away from the airport in Baltimore after our flight from New Orleans. You remarked how Jim just seems to be one of those people whom circumstances always force to do just what they want to do, though they may try to do just as they are told.

PSB: Of course there is a type, of which our photographer is an amusing and lovable example. Your very vehement instructions interest him only mildly, he listens as to a voice afar off, responds by vague suggestions of his own which when rejected by you with vigor, he seems to abandon. Thus when you had instructed him to meet us at the Baltimore airport, insisting that we, the car and the van, ought to meet as centrally and as soon as possible, he mentioned the Norfolk hotel, and you instantly rejected the idea. He went off apparently docile. But somewhere along the turnpike it seems that it became impossible for him to reach the airport. All roads led to the hotel, and at the hotel we met.

I had a manservant once in my house in China of the same type, so race and geography have nothing to do with it. He came to work one morning looking even more languid than usual and upon my question said that his wife had a fever and he had had to tend her all night. Fever turned out to be typhoid and I told him he must take his wife to the hospital at once. He objected on the grounds that people who went to the hospital always died. I said this was untrue because they went there to get well. He listened unbelieving but out of courtesy obeyed. Three days later word came that she was indeed dying. He asked for a week off, went to the hospital in spite of my protest and that of the hospital, and took her home in a riksha. At the end of a week he came back to work, as languid as ever, to report her well and able to cook and wash as usual. East and West, the type persists and always wins.

TFH: Norfolk was fun! But I'll confess I wondered many times what our reception would be in a service town. Here we were trying to raise money for the children born out of wedlock to American servicemen and Asian women. We could have been tarred and feathered and run out of town on a rail in a service town. Our reception, however, was quite different from tar and feathers. We were royally treated. The manager and his wife here had given us a ball previously in Binghamton, New York, so going into a town where they were hosts again was like going home. They had interesting things planned for us but the highlight for us both was luncheon with the captain aboard the USS *Enterprise* and the ensuing tour of that floating city. The captain was wonderful to us. I should have known, however, that as soon as we settled into the car waiting for us you would say:

"I want to see where the ship was made."

After a few hasty telephone calls we were off to the shipyards to satisfy the curiosity of a lady. With this inspiring bit of touristing, a little out of the ordinary, we did some very ordinary sight-seeing. We visited one or two of the old historical houses. Then, of course, we had to see the memorial tomb of the great General MacArthur. I felt a little strange as I walked down halls dedicated to the man who had accomplished so many great things, better than anyone else would have, but who said of our children in Japan:

"We will not speak of these children!"

PSB: I suppose the General realized that the problem of the new Amerasian children was complex, perhaps too complex to face at a time when there were the monstrous tasks of the military occupation of Japan. He must have realized, too, how impossible it was to forbid young American men to seek out girls, especially the charming docile girls of Japan, trained to submit and to please. As for the girls—well, they were not accustomed to men who tried to please them, as well, and perhaps they, too, are not to be blamed for yielding to blandishments. And when communication by language is difficult or impossible, it is natural that the young, male and female, resort to other means.

At any rate, some nine months after the Occupation, I was told that when the first Amerasian baby was born an enthusiastic Japanese radio announcer proclaimed "the first goodwill baby." The command came down that these babies were not to be mentioned and the radio announcer lost his job. Thereafter silence fell. Only at the end of the Occupation did the news burst forth to declare there were two hundred thousand Amerasian children, a figure so enormous that it was instantly denied by the American authorities, who made a research of their own and came up with the revised figure of five thousand, a figure unrealistically low, in the opinion of the Japanese, who said that for most Amerasian births there are no records, since it is seldom that doctors or even midwives attend the mothers. At any rate, the children were born and continue to be born and grow like lonely weeds along a country roadside. The American military policy was to ignore both circumstances and child unless and until a young man thought of marriage. Then he was shipped away to a distant post. There was some reason for this abrupt transference, for the military felt a responsibility to the American family, who might not welcome an Asian member.

Such were my thoughts as we wandered through the memorial building General MacArthur planned for himself.

TFH: Raleigh was next and my outstanding memory is of our meeting with the Governor of North Carolina. We sat in his office for about an hour and chatted while you came on with your usual barrage of questions which he attempted to answer. As we left he offered to call ahead and arrange for us to be received at the Governor's Mansion so that we could see the historic old house. We asked him not to disturb his wife, for we would probably not have time to stop. He expressed his regrets and off we went for a drive. When we rode around the city and passed the Governor's Mansion, however, we promptly decided we must go in, for it was a most unusual edifice, ornate and yet beautiful. We marched right up to the door and asked if we could come in. Although I am sure we took the First Lady of the state by surprise she was all charm and graciousness as she showed us about the house and ordered coffee to be served in the library at the end of our tour. I watched this pleasant lady go about her hostessing duties and I remember thinking to myself what an asset such a wife is to a man in public life. You have said:

"Bless men at the top!"

I follow with:

"Bless their wives!"

PSB: I am never sure whether the wives make the men or the men make the wives. I suppose it is a mutual cooperation. Women like, even long, to be proud of the men they marry. They have the right to such pride, since for most women marriage is still their chosen career. Yet it is worthwhile only when the men they marry are inspiring, growing human beings. When the man fails to be such a person the relationship degenerates on the woman's side into maternalism. No true woman wants to be a mother to her husband. The very idea revolts her. Yet if the man behaves like a child, she is compelled to be a mother to him. This is the explanation, I believe, for what Philip Wylie has so bitterly denounced as "momism." A woman is a "mom" only when the man to whom she is married demands a mother rather than a wife, companion, and partner. We've talked about this before—remember?

The beautiful woman in the Governor's Mansion, of whom you speak so truly, was a happy wife. I can understand why, for, as you say, we had already met the Governor, and I cannot imagine him wanting a mother-wife. He was confident, mature and intelligent, an inspiring person and a successful man. I knew very well what his wife would be, even before I saw her.

TFH: All I can remember about the drive from Raleigh to Savannah is that it was long. The day was drab, if you will remember, and it was on that drive that we started this book. We established a pattern quickly—short spurts of mental gymnastics (a game of Scrabble or a sight-seeing jaunt) followed by hours of writing furiously, you and I sitting in the back of your big car. First I write and then read to you—then you write and read to me. What fun! I wholeheartedly recommend "Dialogues" as a great travel "game." Time passed so quickly we moved from one place to another scarcely knowing we had begun to do so. How lucky for you, and the world, the fate that decreed you were to be a writer!

PSB: The question most often asked me is:
"What made you know you were a writer?"

However often this question is asked, it always confounds me. How did I know—when did I know? I do not know how but it was always. When I reach back into the horizons of the past, I could already read, and ever since I could read I have wanted to write and did write.

Analytically, I suppose, one must say that a writer is created, as all else is created, according to formula. The ingredients are a compound of talent and energy, talent being the chemistry and energy being the physics. Chemistry and physics must be in proper proportion to each other if the reaction is to occur in the positive form of creativity. A person may have remarkable talent but if he has not sufficient energy to use the talent, he will never become a successful writer, and his fate will be frustration.

TFH: Savannah was a pleasant city for us. We enjoyed its old homes with gingerbread ironwork and streets laid out with square parks at intersections. I remember one of the houses there particularly well. It was being restored to its original grandeur by a young man, proprietor of an antique shop. When we were about to leave, after our tour of his shop, we saw an oval table in the entrance hall. It stood like a large pillbox on legs with a glass top, lined with velvet. How like us to decide then and there that this was the perfect table in which to display the Nobel Prize gold medal! We announced we must have it, bought it on the spot, and took it with us in the back of the van. It waits now in the Foundation building for the time to come when finally it can house its treasure. I'm sure the great Alfred Nobel would be happy if he could know that his honor, bestowed on what was called a young upstart of a woman, was now to help raise money to take care of the world's most needy children. A career that started thirty-six years ago working for greater understanding, friendship and peace between the two great cultures of her childhood in *East Wind: West Wind* is striving toward this very same goal today. A radio interviewer in New York City recently said that there was really only one person in the world today qualified to give advice on affairs in Asia. "How strange," he said, "that no President, no general, no ambassador, has ever called her to Washington and asked for her help!"

We saw these two cultures of East and West united in that Southern city, if you will remember, in the four young sons of the dance studio manager, indeed in the manager himself, who is partly Chinese. His grandmother was one-fourth Chinese and while he doesn't look very Asian, his sons certainly do.

It was in Savannah also that some crank called a radio show and caused a great stir among city officials and news reporters by saying that you, Pearl Buck, are a Communist.

PSB: The landscape of the Deep South made me sad. I tried to analyze my depression and found that it was first of all caused by the gray festoons of Spanish moss on the trees. I know that this moss is considered by some people a characteristic beauty of the Southern scene, but to me it was only depressing. The moss is so gray, so clinging, so possessive. A living tree is gay, its green changing from the jade of early spring to midsummer richness, and then to the gold and brown of autumn. But the long ragged strands of gray moss rob the tree of all color and it becomes a ghost, in a haunted forest of ghosts. You remember that we toyed with the idea that if we lived in the South we would set up a movement to strip the trees of gray moss and set them free again.

This gray moss became symbolic for me of a certain atmosphere of sadness in the beautiful South, which I felt but could not define—something old and gray, something pervading, unyielding, bigoted, devitalizing the spirit and stifling growth. It focused suddenly and sharply one day, though only for a moment, in the old, tiresome accusation that I was a Communist. So absurd is this accusation, so ignorant, so impossible—I a Communist?—I who warned against Communism so steadfastly as I saw it coming into a distracted, war-torn China in 1921? I who in 1927 nearly lost my life at the hands of a vengeful Communist army as it arrived triumphant in the Chinese city of Nanking where I was then living? No, it is not I who am the menace. It is the mind of that man who called, anonymously, the cowardly embittered mind of a person who hates anyone who believes in justice, even in the South, and who denounces as Communist all who disagree with him. As the gray pall hangs over the green growing trees of the South, the pall of bigotry hangs over the people.

You ask for my impressions, especially of Florida?

Let me remember! A broad general impression is that of growth. I feel Florida stretching its muscles and its mind. It is a physical growth but that physical growth is impelled by mental growth. Mind and soul, Florida is ready to grow beyond present imagination. True, it has the limitations of the past, which are still quite clear. It has to make fresh ground. Symbolically and literally I saw this ground being made along the coastlines. Out of the surrounding seas I saw great dredging machines dig up the bottom sand and pile it into new islands and new beaches. The seawater soaks out of the new land, it grows firm and hard, houses are built upon it, people move in, grass is sown, flowers bloom, a city is enlarged. I felt the same push toward growth among the people, especially the young people. More than I have felt anywhere else in the United States thus far I felt the great hunger of the young people in Florida for new ideas, new areas of work and imagination, new knowledge. This hunger grows of course out of discontent with present situations. Let me give one example.

It was late afternoon in a certain inland city. I will not give the name of the city because it is rather a sad place—Spanish moss again! I felt its sadness when I entered its streets. Cities have their atmosphere and I am susceptible to atmosphere. I remember thinking, that afternoon in my hotel rooms, that surely something was wrong. I remember looking out over the city roofs, and wondering how it would be possible to live there. Something—something was wrong. The air was listless. The people lacked vitality, not physical but spiritual. I wondered if we realize that physical vitality is always based on vitality of the spirit?

The telephone rang and I answered it. Three young people were downstairs in the lobby. They represented a high school newspaper. Would I give them a few minutes? I hesitated. My schedule was already arranged and very tight indeed—press conferences, radio, television—I had been traveling and needed a few hours of rest before the ball in the evening. Then suddenly I decided. It would be a good chance for me to discover whether I was right in my judgment of the city. If the young people too were listless and dull I would inquire of them the cause and so learn what was wrong.

"Let them come up," I said.

In a few minutes I heard a knock at the door and I opened it. There stood two boys, one tall, the other short. Between them was a plump young girl with a pleasant open face.

"Come in," I said.

They came in. I noticed that the short boy had a tape recorder. It was a good one and it was in good order. He set it ready to record, saying that he hoped I would not object to being recorded, since he had definite questions to ask and wanted to have my answers definite. They all had definite questions. Sitting side by side on the sofa and facing me, I was impressed by their air of competence and common sense. They were on good terms with each other, and had evidently decided before they came exactly what they wanted from me. The short boy took a paper from his breast pocket and proceeded to fire away. They were good questions, and they covered the world scene well enough so that I saw that he was following world affairs. I had not always seen the same interest in his elders. Nor did he accept superficial answers from me. He did not want simplification. He wanted to know why we were engaged in war in Vietnam and what I thought our chances there were. He wanted to know why Indonesia objected to Malaysia. And what did I think the effect of Nehru's death would be in India? Was there any chance of the Tibetans regaining their country? Did I believe that in the long run Japan would continue to side with the West? What if China emerged as a powerful modern nation sooner than we thought possible?

I found myself put through a real examination, with reasons required for every opinion. The tall boy was interested in art and its relation to modern life, and the girl wanted to know about literature and the ways of writers. They deserved the most honest answers that I could give, and I gave them my best. These were not reporters working for a living. They were young people who wanted to know, and there is no more exciting experience in life than to discover such persons, young or old. The hope of the future lies in their hands. But how did it come about that this depressing city produced these young people?

"Now it is my turn," I said at last. "I have a few questions of my own."

I told them then exactly how I felt about their city. It was unjust of me, perhaps, I told them, since I had been there so short a time, but I felt the air of the city oppressive.

"And I don't mean just your paper mill, either," I said.

It was true there was a paper mill in the city as there seems to be in several cities in Florida and these mills give out a strange sulphurous odor that adds its own miasmic effect to the Spanish moss.

"It's something else," I said. "It shows in the faces of the people here. They look as though they had nothing to look forward to, as if today had been exactly like yesterday and as if they knew tomorrow would be the same as today."

I might have opened a door into another world. The three looked at each other and at me.

"Let's tell her the truth," the short boy said.

"Why not?" the tall boy replied.

"It's like this—" the girl began.

For two hours they told me what was wrong with their town. They knew everything. They knew about graft and corruption at the highest levels. They knew where money had been collected and spent and not for the purposes for which it had been collected. They had facts on men in the seats of power. These young people were literal-minded, unsentimental, condemnatory, angry, and fiercely idealistic. They did not believe, they would not believe, that such conditions had to be. They understood politics but they did not accept the notion that political life must be corrupt.

"We've got to understand that it pays to choose honest men," the short boy said.

"We don't have to be robbed, generation after generation," the tall boy said.

The two boys were even more positive, more angry, more determined, than the girl. She sighed now and then.

"Our parents live in a rut," she said. "All our elders live in the same rut. They're afraid to try anything new, because their jobs are tied in with the corruption. I only hope and pray that we don't get into that same rut. I hope we don't get afraid, like they are. Maybe we're partly the reason they're afraid. Maybe it's getting married and having children and the bills to pay."

"No," the short boy said. "It's being too lazy to know what's going on. It's being too lazy to think and to act—in time. It's being afraid to do anything."

Their fury, I discovered, was centered in the fact that their county only the day before had lost accreditation for its high schools. This meant that they, the young people, could not hope to get into colleges outside their own state. These were young people who wanted to go to the best colleges in the country. They were deeply angry at what had happened, especially as they felt that public funds had been spent in questionable ways. They knew exactly what those funds were and how they had been wasted.

I sat in silence, listening while they unfolded to me the

story of their city. They loved the place as one loves one's parents, whatever they may be, and they hated the place as one hates one's parents when they are less than one longs to have them be. Who of us does not remember? But the heartening was in the very fact of their love and their hate. If only the fire did not die down too soon, crushed by the demands of life! I found myself hoping that they would not grow old too quickly, would not marry too soon and too soon be overcome by the burdens of babies and bills and fears of losing the precious job. Perhaps it was this fear, already casting its shadow over the young girl, that made her murmur again, "Oh, I hope we don't get into the same old rut!"

"I hope and pray," I said.

They went away at last. I have not been able to forget them. They were stars in the darkness, they were angels singing in the night. I cannot bear to think that stars may be quenched and singing be silenced. I wonder if it must be so?

This incident came near the end of the tour. We had traveled from city to city, weaving our way across the state, north and west so different from the south and east, inland so very different from the seacoast, such contrasts of ugliness and beauty. I was especially interested in the Negro people of Florida. They are very black, very beautiful, and they bear themselves with a dignity that seems natural to them. I must find out if they come ancestrally from a special part of Africa. They have fine features and they move with grace. Their hands are delicately made. They are aristocratic in appearance. I had not seen them before. I was impressed by their relationship to the white people. There is a distance between the two races, it is obvious, but it seemed to me not angry. There is a good deal of quiet integration taking place. I spoke at several high schools, by special request of the young people, and it was an interesting contrast to speak to thousands of listening white faces on one day and to thousands of black faces the next day, for those schools were still segregated. Yet aside from the color there was no difference. Each group was respectful, interested and enthusiastic, each group was cleanly and neatly dressed and well behaved. They will work out their own equalities and cooperation, I feel sure. All the same, I found I could not give the same speech to the white and to the black. I felt strangely apologetic and indeed inferior before the dark people. I felt I was put in an embarrassing position because I was white. I do not enjoy feeling inferior or embarrassed. I am not accustomed to such feelings, and I hope that next time I do not look at a solid white audience or a solid black one. I don't like being in the wrong.

III

TFH: And now we have really worked our way back to the beginning, or is it forward to the beginning of this book? Our visits to the various cities in Florida took on a definite pattern broken by only a few unusual events. We visited Silver Springs, you will remember, and while we were entertained for the day you learned all about how to milk rattlesnakes, and it was there that the green parrot joined our entourage, a twenty-five-year-old bird with the ability to speak Spanish and English quite fluently, and a friendly easy way of winning people over.

PSB: Speaking of snakes, I am reminded of the two cobras who were part of the cast when the film of *The Guide* was being made in India. It was my first experience of living with snakes. True, there were snakes enough in my Chinese childhood. In those days I particularly disliked the tree snakes. I being a tree climber myself, it was disconcerting to reach a favorite crotch in a tree and discover a snake curled there. Invariably I followed the ancient Chinese proverb, "Of the thirty-six ways of escape, the best is to run away." There was also that long thin green snake which enjoyed living in our bamboo grove, and the poisonous green and dangerous little mountain snake that springs out to deliver death upon the traveler unaware. Chinese snakes in general showed a fondness for climbing, and more than once we found them climbing the stairs to the second floor of the house.

Here in my American home I have avoided the dam that holds back the waters of the small lake at the foot of the hill, for the great rocks there are the favorite haunts of water snakes. I am told these are harmless, but I cannot believe malice is not contained in that shape. Once I came inadvertently upon a long narrow black snake at the door of the camellia house. It was early spring and the day was one of those gay bright intervals between March winds and April rains. I could not stay indoors, and now and again fled my desk on some outdoor pretext or other. On one such sortie I felt it necessary to search for a late camellia and so came face to face with the snake. Face to face it was, for the creature lifted its small head to gaze at me with such evil that I ran back to my study, locked the door, and did not leave my desk all day.

It was the two cobras in India, however, which crystallized my knowledge and feeling upon the subject of serpents. One cobra, a huge one, was a lovely blond beige. She—it was impossible to believe her anything but female—had the temperament of a blonde. It was a cool, remote temperament, detached, apparently, from everyone, until roused to fury. She loved only her keeper and would obey no other, although she had bitten him so often that he was as full of venom as she was and therefore immune to her attacks. True, she was defanged from time to time, but one never knew when the dangerous stuff secreted itself again. Indeed, so poisoned was the keeper that he must be careful, he told me, never to let his blood get into the open wound of another person lest that one die as though by a cobra's venom.

It was the duty of the blond cobra on stage to rise out of her round basket and sway to the music of a flute while the young Indian beauty danced before her. No command of the director, however, could move that willful serpent. Only her keeper, coaxing and loving, could persuade her to effort. Even this sometimes was not enough. Then pretending to be angry at her indifference he pinched her tail for punishment. Up she rose, her spine straightening until she stood three and even four feet tall, and, slowly, her eyes fixed on her keeper, she unfolded her silvery hood. There was a deadly beauty in that small haughty head, the tiny snub-nosed profile, the cold, shining small black eyes. I was frightened while I admired. I wanted to run away and could not. It was a relief when the dance was over and the creature shut into her basket again.

The black male cobra was another sort, not beautiful. He appeared on stage only for an instant when he was supposed to be killed. I say supposed, for the truth was that no one would kill him. Tradition in India says that cobras live as lifelong mates, and if one of a pair is killed the other will find where the killer hides and deal him the blow of death. I ponder the question of why the serpent is detested and so universally and instinctively that the exception, a person who likes snakes, is considered strange. I think myself into the body of a snake, having no hands or feet, no fin or wing, and wonder if such construction does not create malevolence. I thought of all this the day we bought the green parrot in Silver Springs.

TFH: Later in Miami we got the African gray parrot, only one year old, and not yet trained. It was fun to see the two birds get acquainted and they gave us quite a lot of pleasure. I'm sure we must have presented a strange picture traveling around with two birds. They now have a fine time at the Foundation, shouting their parrot quips and laughter.

I remember especially the beauty of the gardens we saw in St. Petersburg and Tampa and the hospitality displayed by our hosts in those cities. I think without a moment's hesitation we both will agree that the most beautiful and successful ball was held in St. Petersburg. The people, all in formal evening dress, stood in line by the hundreds. We were both anxious to get back to the office and work, however, and were quite impatient with the business of stop and go connected with long trips. I don't know what it was we expected to find when we returned to our Foundation house, but I'm sure it was not what we actually found. Dust, dirt, ladders, tools, plaster, demolition and construction were going on at the same time on different floors. I remember you walking through the rooms looking like a small child, eyes huge with the utter and complete horror of chaos. I remember the wee, quiet, almost lost sound of your voice as you said:

"Well, we've come this far and we must go on." Things seem to have crept along at a snail's pace for the past seven months but as I look back on all the things we have accomplished it does seem unbelievable.

Yes, there is no time now to look back, we must forge ahead. We have a force in Korea, our work well begun there. An employee in our office in Philadelphia and volunteers are working for us all over this vast United States. We have thousands of children for whom we must provide a future. Time can mar a child beyond repair. You have said, "The years between birth and adulthood are swift and few." They are! Hours blend into day, noon and on into night. They become weeks, months, and years, relentlessly. The horror of each passing day for these children burns within me as I know it does in you. And so . . . we go on. City by city, state by state, ball by ball, we travel throughout our country telling Americans in all walks of life of the plight of these forsaken Amerasians. And they do respond.

After only a few weeks we set forth on our second tour and we are now in Texas, our Lone Star state, and only last night in San Antonio the manager of the local dance studio pledged full support for the thirty-five children of the Company D Orphanage. They were good to us in that city, striving to show us all of the points of interest in our short two-day stay. As we enter Houston this bright and sunny day I look forward to returning to San Antonio. What was most special for you there?

PSB: There was a special charm about the city of San Antonio. When I reflect, I feel that it is its link with the past. Few cities in our country have this link. They seem to spring newborn out of plains or mountains. But San Antonio has kept its relics. There in the Alamo, the great cathedral of the past, one can learn of the Spanish first settlers, and of the men who came to join them and of the bitter fight to wrench the land away. It was a struggle between Mexican and American finally, and at first the Americans lost, only one escaping to tell the tragic story. Then the reserves fought again to reclaim what had been lost.

To wander through the old buildings, their walls indestructibly thick, is to slip back across the centuries. And what a contrast this provides for the most modern medical center, where specially trained men investigate the physical and mental hazards of space travel! As you know, wherever we go, I insist upon visiting any center for space travel. In San Antonio it was something new, this medical aspect. Remember the young men, all volunteers, who were patiently carrying on experiments in sealed cells simulating spacecraft? One young man, after I had passed, wanted me to return and when I did so, he asked for my autograph and sent me, through a sealed conveyor, this poem:

PICASSO'S HUMAN COMEDY

A Calliope is cluttering my lawn
With clatter music out of time and rhythm,
Strewing clowns about the terraces
And scattering their ragged laughter with them.
Although I cannot see those clownish faces,
I'm sure some misplaced circus, past its season
Is crowding in among the snapping dragons;
A circus left without a touring reason
Up among the clatter of a steam calliope.
But no matter how I strain to see,
No matter how the window faces me,
An eager clown is there to face my eyes.
And the only circus vision left to me
Is that I see through her reflected eyes.*

I remember so well the strange scene of that space vehicle in which a young man sat confined, a boy really, not more than twenty, and he was writing poetry!

Among many interesting parts of this complex medical research, however, two engaged me most. The first was weightlessness and the second was the possible uses of algae and duckweed. Weightlessness, it seems, has an effect upon

* Printed with permission of the author, Curtis L. Harris.

the circulatory system. The medical researchers were trying to reproduce the state of weightlessness, and have discovered, after prolonged submersion in water, that simply staying in bed provides the best simulation for human beings. This discovery accounts to some degree for the decision to get postoperative cases out of bed as quickly as possible. It was interesting to see in the film that was shown us how the astronauts navigate themselves when weightless. They seem to swim, arms and legs moving. Yet since there is no force to oppose, they would still remain motionless, did they not push themselves off from some stationary object. Care must be taken not to push too hard, for they may strike some other object with the same energy. The astronauts report that the state of weightlessness is pleasant. One feels free of all oppressions. Since our visit to this space center of course we know still more about weightlessness, for now man has floated in space, attached to his vehicle only by a lifeline.

Of algae and duckweed, what interested me was their oxygen-producing propensities. Algae is valuable as a food, and we were shown large flat pills made of algae which we were told could sustain life. But even more important is the fact that algae create oxygen and carry away carbon dioxide and thus provide an atmosphere. Will it be possible some day, I wonder, to create an atmosphere on the moon, for example, by the use of algae? I put the question to an astronaut and he did not find it strange.

TFH: Frankly, I enjoyed our dinner at the Petroleum Club, for it gave us a chance to see all of Houston at the same time. The entire city stretched out before us in miles and miles of lights like a twinkling, glittering Christmas tree forever changing.

You probed into every situation with your usual questions and the scene took my mind years back to San Francisco and the first Christmas I had ever spent alone. Young and in a strange city, I had not had a chance to find work before the holiday season set in and I had begun to lose heart as my funds dwindled. I could acord no Christmas, really, and being alone for the holiday for the first time was depressing. I consoled myself by sitting at the Top of the Mark with the one drink I could afford. Suddenly my heart lifted. I told myself that the wonderful city spread out before me was my Christmas tree, all mine. I went out the next day and landed the best job I had in San Francisco. It was a strange experience for me now to sit, in the present, and have the scene take me back to that earlier time and place. Perhaps I'm beginning to understand your detached air. I was snapped back to the present by your question about visiting NASA.

PSB: I was impatient to see the great NASA installation where astronauts are trained, at this moment for the projected trip to the moon. We put off until another visit the famous Cow Palace and the new domed stadium. The first morning found us in NASA, and there we met the astronauts face to face. Colonel John Glenn I had met before at a dinner at the White House in President Kennedy's time, and now we met the others, those who had been in space and those preparing to go. They showed us the sort of vehicles they had used, or planned to use. It was fascinating enough to study these crafts, but what interested me most was the men themselves.

"Are you not afraid when you contemplate going into space?" we asked.

"Call it fear," one replied for the others. "Each time I watch a great rocket sent off from Cape Kennedy, I am afraid, for I know that surely the day will come when I'll go up in one of them. Yet go I will and must."

Riding a tethered bomb, is the way Jimmy, our photographer, put it!

What have these astronauts in common? Without exception they are clean-cut, well-groomed, good-looking. They are of medium build and self-controlled. They are trained to such perfection that they know as much about their instruments as the men who made them, or as well, one of them said, as the tools in their own homes. But there is more than that. There is an air of detachment about them, as though, knowing space, they can never come back entirely to earth. Their eyes are distant, as though accustomed to horizons more remote than those we know. They have already become dwellers in the universe.

And their wives? Pretty girls, all young, all busy about their children—and waiting for their husbands to come home again!

TFH: I don't think that in my wildest imagination anything could have pleased me more than meeting those young people, our astronauts and their wives. Four of them met us to begin our tour.

It amused me to see the look of surprise on the faces of our guides when you began to ask questions. At both the Aero Space Medical Center and at NASA the remark was the same.

"We have conducted these tours for scientific groups but never have we had such intelligent questions asked of us."

It gives me a great sense of pride when these remarks are made to me behind your back. When I repeat them to you your remark is always:

"They must have had very stupid people going through there."

Later at a brunch arranged for us by the NASA Public Relations Department we met the commander of the astronauts. It was a well-arranged affair with everyone bursting with questions to ask you ranging from *East Wind: West Wind* to *The Joy of Children*. With your determined-to-know expression on your face, however, I knew the shoe would be on the other foot. You sat on the corner of the porch opening off the sitting room and asked questions to your heart's content, and I could tell you were enjoying yourself thoroughly.

When I discovered, hours after our visit there, that our table at the ball was filled with astronauts, I was pleased. The dancers in the show were among the best I have ever seen and the conversation at our table kept me so busy that the evening flew and before I knew it, it was gone. The young man sitting to my left was one of those scheduled to go up in the near future. I asked many questions of him and found him not only willing but eager to talk. He told me of his experience as a jet pilot and that the astronauts were all required to be engineers as well. I could not but admire the courage I found in him as we talked.

"I know when I go that the best brains in this country are behind me," he told me. "There is apprehension, of course. I suppose you could call it fear, but I know I will go."

Today we ride from Houston to Tyler. I look ahead with great pleasure to Houston next year. I shall watch our space program with renewed interest, faith and pride. I wish that everyone in our country could have the opportunity to learn what we learned on that trip to Houston.

One other thing I have learned in Texas is about Prohibition. It is better to buy a drink across the bar than to have to take a whole bottle everywhere one goes. Remember how strange it was to see people, all dressed up in their finery, come through the receiving line clutching their bottles? Remember how much and how furiously they drink so they need not be compelled to carry a half-empty bottle out?

PSB: Yes, I remember! Never before have I seen so many nice old ladies and sweet young girls drunk. You refused them as dance partners, in spite of their frank pursuit of you, because, you said, they simply were not able to dance when drunk. And you were quick to see when a drunk would cut in when I was dancing, and ordered Jimmy to rescue me.

The difficulty, of course, lies in our American localism. In Texas one county may decide to prohibit liquor while the county next to it allows it. Each county is a law to itself. This independence is unrealistic, for those who want to drink spend their money in the wet county. Yet this lack of realism extends throughout American life. Each state has its own laws which may entirely negate by contradiction the laws of the next state. Our foreign policy reflects this unrealistic behavior.

We still do not understand the necessity of life in our modern world. No nation can act independently of others. Cooperation, organization, negotiation, compromise in the best sense, is the only realism today upon this crowded globe, the home we share with many peoples.

TFH: Our hotel in Fort Worth was the same one where Kennedy spent his last night. At the press conference I felt strange when a reporter told us that yours was the very bed. It was a comfortable old hotel, elegant in a quiet way—high ceilings and wood-paneled walls, forming wide spacious rooms. It had mirrors, reflecting crystal chandeliers that set off the massive furniture. Our rooms were called the Will Rogers Suite. They looked as though they must have been furnished for their namesake, comfortable, masculine and simple in concept.

PSB: Will Rogers was my friend. I first heard of him when I was living in Nanking, China. It was in the autumn, I think, of 1932, or perhaps 1931. He was in Shanghai, on a world tour, and he had asked me if he could travel the two hundred miles up the Yangtse River valley and visit me. I did not know who he was, but my publishers in New York had sent me a clipping from *The New York Times*, in which he said of *The Good Earth*, "It is not only the greatest book about a people ever written but the best book of our generation. So go get this and read it!"

Such praise made me feel shy, and I rather dreaded meeting him, although at the same time I wanted to see what sort of person he was, who could so speak of my book. Alas, he could not come. That was the year when the Yangtse River rose to phenomenal heights. Much of our city was under water and the railroad from Shanghai was impassable. A year later I was in New York and Will Rogers came to call upon me in my suite in the famous old Murray Hill Hotel, now gone. He brought his attractive wife with him and we had a valuable hour together—our last, as it turned out, for he was killed in an airplane accident before ever we could meet again.

Yes, it was strange to see the remembered face, smiling in its usual kind way, when I entered the hotel in Fort Worth. A larger than life-sized portrait, in color, faced the door and welcomed me.

I, too, felt strange when I thought the suite we were in had been the one President Kennedy had used just before the assassination. There was still a pall over Dallas, two days later, but then it focused there in the rooms where we sat. The tragedy of his death had hung over us more and more deeply as we approached Dallas, and in Fort Worth it became unbearable. How could I sleep in that room where he had passed his last night? It was a beautiful room, the furniture of the finest and a great bed in the middle of it.

I had a lecture to give that evening at the Country Club, you remember, the proceeds to go to the Foundation. I had prepared a panorama of the events in history which have led inexorably to the present situation in Asia, and though the material is as familiar to me as my own life, I could not escape the oppressive sadness that pervaded me. I could not eat the delicious dinner that was served and I dreaded returning to the hotel. Suddenly a telephone message came from the reporter who had given us the information. It was false, he said. Upon inquiry, he said, he discovered that mine was not the suite where Kennedy had slept his last night.

Was it or was it not? If it was, it is unlikely that the hotel would say so. It was on the thirteenth floor, too—lucky that I am not superstitious! At any rate, I decided to believe the correction and I slept well enough in the huge bed.

It was inevitable, however, that all conversations during the two days in Dallas tended toward the assassination. People have not recovered, and will never recover, wholly. Their self-confidence has been shaken. Such a deed could be done, was done, in their handsome city. They pointed out the exact spot, the fatal window, the route to the hospital. Business was at a standstill for many days after the tragedy, they said, and for months was at only half its usual level. People had no heart for buying more than the few essentials. There was no joy anywhere. Even yet, and perhaps forever, the old ebullience is gone.

Yes, Dallas itself is a handsome city, and its citizens, too, are handsome people. Remember how we spoke of the ball that night? Tall men and women in evening dress, the dancing better than usual, and everything done with style and flair— all this gave an impression of sophistication and worldliness in the best sense beyond anything we had found elsewhere in Texas. Kind and good people we found everywhere—very charming men, I discovered. What was it that soldier boy told us about the girls in Korea, something to the effect that they think our American men all come from Texas? Is that a compliment or isn't it? At any rate, let us assume that it is.

This was not my first visit to Texas, however. I went there once, some years ago. How and why? The question may be asked since I am never a tourist. I do not go anywhere in the world merely to see. I have no criticism of tourists, for certainly merely to see is a delightful occupation. But I have never had time for it or so I make the excuse. When I travel, it is to participate in something. That first visit to Dallas, for example, was immediately after the Second World War. I was writing a novel about scientists, as you know, and specifically about a scientist who had to decide whether to drop an atomic bomb. *Command the Morning* was the result of my own absorption in the whole subject of scientific responsibility. In order to get my facts right, I had visited a number of atomic installations, among them Los Alamos. That in itself was an experience. We left Albuquerque after breakfast one desert-bright summer morning and after a motor trip we climbed into an aircraft slightly larger than a bathtub, and floated up the mountain to the installation to hear the story of the atomic bomb that was made there.

When I came down again from the mountain, I looked at a map, saw how near Texas was, remembered that I had never set foot on that vast stretch of American soil, and not knowing whether I would ever be as near again, wanderer though I am, I went to Dallas. I became absorbed in that city and I remembered its skyscraper towers rising symbolically out of the smooth surrounding country. Why do people build skyscrapers when there is more than enough land to spare? It is, I imagine, a necessity for contrast, a compulsion for the upward thrust of the spirit rising above the uniformity of everyday life. I mention the Dallas I saw in those years, because it seemed to me then a city almost devoid of culture. Money was evident, but the desert was pervasive. But I remember, too, visiting the famous Nieman-Marcus department store and finding there a distinguished man, unexpected, I must confess, who waited for me in his office and took time to show me about the beautiful premises. He told me of his dreams for Dallas, and I remember them, for some of them have come true. He, too, spoke of the desert, and was well aware of its emptiness.

TFH: It seemed more than coincidence to have that young man approach us in Fort Worth and say, "My daughter was born in Korea on the twenty-third of last month. Can you help to get them here or me there?"

A man in a high position in that very city, when approached to buy a $5 ticket to our ball, had said, "This is not a local problem. I will not give money to anything and have it go out of our city!"

Not local? If we even hinted that any town, USA, didn't send as many young men abroad as any other town, its citizens would be insulted. By the same token if we so much as insinuated that all of the young men from any town USA were abnormal again the citizens would be insulted. Yet over and over, "This is not a local problem. I can't help." They wouldn't dare to say that to us! They do say it, though, when a committee member tries to sell a ticket. Ah, sweet mystery of life. . . .

This young man told the same old story:

"I met her one night at one of my buddies' hooch." (A hooch is a small mud hut in which some of our GIs live with their girl of the hour.) "I had just arrived in Korea a few days earlier. I was terribly lonely. I had had no word from home for months. You don't know how lonely you can get over there away from everything. Anyway, I got tired of just sitting around with the guys so when this buddy who had been there for awhile invited me to visit him and his girl at their hooch, I went. That's where I met my girl. She is his girl's girlfriend."

"Was she a prostitute?" I couldn't help asking.

"No! Well, yes . . . She did charge me. But I lived with her for a whole year. All that's changed now. We got a bigger hooch. She is a wonderful girl."

My next question was only natural. "Why didn't you marry her?"

"I tried, but they wouldn't let me. I couldn't show that I had $500 to bring her back to the United States."

PSB: The problem of the child born out of wedlock cannot be solved basically because the two persons, man and woman, are themselves problems, and therefore they produce a third problem when they produce the child. The child is our concern, but the first concern is that he not be born, or at least not born in such circumstances. Take this man, for example. He is not a man but a boy. He is twenty years old, yes—but he is a child, immature, ill-educated, lacking in self-confidence, lost. His parents, he told us, you remember, are divorced. He felt himself unloved, unwanted. He was searching for what he had never had, but he was not hopeful about himself. Though he looked clean and his uniform was neat, he was not at all handsome and he knew it. Shy, uneasy, retiring, it was obvious that he expected little happiness in life. He was ripe for any woman who gave him consideration, gentleness, a technique of deference, all that in which the Asian woman is so well trained.

Now take the woman he described to us, who had borne his child. Yes, she is a woman. She is twenty-four years old to his twenty. It is a severe age difference in any country, but in Asia where the girl matures early, the difference is even greater than in the West. It is the greater, too, because this woman became a prostitute when she was in her early teens, perhaps as early as twelve.

For she, too, was an unloved child. Her parents were poor. They lived in a village and farmed a small piece of land. There were several children, too many, and the sons were considered more important than the daughters, since girls go to another family at marriage. When this girl was still a child, she was sent by third-class train to the big city, one among many such girls. When they descended, procurers were waiting for them with promises. So she went to the brothel and served her time. Her big chance came when the Americans arrived, Americans with money. They were boys eager for sex, and sex was now her profession. There was no wile, no temptation, no form of stimulation, which she did not know, and she used all. Yet underneath it there was something real. She, too, wanted love and a home, a place where she belonged and someone of her own. She made a hooch into a home, temporary it is true, but with dreams of permanence. Here they set up housekeeping, American man and Asian woman. She learned to cook the dishes he liked best. She took care of him and devoted herself to him alone.

Yes, he paid her, but not always in cash. He brought articles from the PX and she sold them in the black market and used the money thriftily to support them both. It was almost like marriage, but not quite. She had not established the final hold. That came when she was pregnant.

You see how the story builds? It is the story of eighty thousand prostitutes in Korea alone—and the story, too, of thousands of American boys. I say boys, for the wife of an Air Force officer told me in Dayton, Ohio, only yesterday that on Okinawa where her husband was stationed for several years, they lived near Shacktown, and daily as she came and went she saw the young American boys, eighteen, nineteen, twenty, sometimes only seventeen, crowding into that sad area. And another officer's wife told me that when her husband was stationed in a small Japanese town, they used to walk in the side alleys in the evening, where the houses were open to the streets, and there the young American boys were again, always the very young.

And you remember that charming man again in Dayton, who told us of his stay in Tientsin during his three and a half years of military service in China. He himself lived for a year with a Chinese girl, but luckily had no child. He told us what

I have never heard said before, and I will repeat it here, for Americans should know it. He told us of the shocking behavior of the American military in and about Tientsin, during the period, and at that place, the most important and sensitive in the whole world just then, for it was when the Communists were threatening to take over China. It was essential that the Chinese people be on our side in that gateway area. They decided, not for the Communists, but against us. Reason? The American in Dayton said:

"Quite frankly, the Chinese people around us did not want the Communists, but they said our men were so undisciplined and were guilty of such unbearable behavior that they felt the Communists could not be worse."

TFH: Let's go back to Dallas and the successful, beautiful ball! As a matter of fact everything in Dallas was big and beautiful. The ball was especially so. The people were elegantly dressed and they appeared to be at least a full foot taller than any crowd we have seen so far. Dallasites are different from the average Texan. They seemed more sophisticated, cultured and worldly-wise, perhaps more mature is the term I'm seeking. We discussed it and decided that they were perhaps second-generation rich, having had their money long enough to know how to handle it. You even suggested that perhaps it was the Nieman-Marcus department store that had brought much of the culture into Dallas, as though the people were striving to live up to this great merchant. Who knows why? The fact of the matter is, they handle themselves better, drink less and are in general better behaved by far, than the average person we saw in Texas. We have discussed often the fact that dancing is very revealing of the character of the people doing it. In Dallas they even danced well. We didn't see any of the undisciplined teen-aged dances. Sophisticated people do not do ungraceful dances. Dallas was indeed a pleasure.

I remember Texas so well from years before when, traveling from east to west or vice versa. I would dread the Texas state line because from there on one could drive for days and seem to get nowhere. I could see farther and see less in that state than anywhere I had ever been, it seemed. After I lived there for a time and began to know the people, I realized the charm of the place. But then, isn't that true of any spot on the globe? One arrives and notices first the geography, and it is "a place"—then one notices the people, and it becomes "a thing" —then one becomes involved with their personalities, and geography disappears and it becomes a state of mind, just as happiness is not a place or thing but a state of mind. But even those personalities can convey mistaken impressions sometimes.

Our young men go to Korea, for example, and are met by beautiful, forward young girls. They wear Western dresses and have lovely faces and smartly styled hair. They greet our GIs, often boys of eighteen, scarcely to be called men, with frank, open proposals of sex. A member of our Board of Governors who visited Korea recently told us of the sixteen- or seventeen-year-old girl who came up to his table in a restaurant, flashed a pure angelic smile, called him "Papa San" and announced brightly:

"Me sex maniac! Wanta swing?"

Our boys, most of them from Smalltown, U.S.A., are, of course, unaccustomed to such frankness and assume that this is the Asian way of doing things. They remember the four-thousand-year-old culture of whose history they know very little, other than war lords and concubines and geishas, and they take the attitude of "When in Rome, do as the Romans do," and act accordingly. They do and say things with a freedom they would not think of expressing in the United States, and they think they are being "Asian."

On the other hand, the girls, most of them from farms and villages of Korea, with little or no real education, have scant knowledge of things American. What they do know of American girls they have learned from motion pictures made in this country and from the movie magazines. They study the photographs of our "sex idols" and watch the torrid scenes in our films, and think that this is American and that, in order to feel at home, our American men must have this atmosphere. They make themselves up to look like our movie stars, learn what GI slang they can, often limited to words of the four-letter variety, don high heels and hair spray, and think that they are being "American."

Out of this basic misunderstanding when two cultures meet, our new people are born—the product of a state of mind. Case in point?

TFH: The return from that Texas tour was pleasant all the way but we seemed most impressed by our two stopping points. St. Louis was impressive as always and in our one full day there we rushed around to see everything. We did take one side trip, however, and it was fun. We went to Alton, Illinois, the birthplace of our Jimmy, and visited his aunt, the Mother Superior in a convent there. We had never been inside a convent. Bright and early one morning we were off with great enthusiasm on another trek to satisfy the curiosity of a lady! I remember thinking how strange that the daughter of a missionary had never been inside a convent.

PSB: Cities have an atomosphere, each its own, and none
is more special than St. Louis. I had visited there once before,
but that time to meet Arthur Compton and in his powerful
presence, I forgot the city—or did not notice it. This time I
could only remember him, for he is dead. Yet the memory is
strong. He had been ill, and with premonitions of the end, I
had gone to see him. The change in him was evident. The old
buoyancy was no more, though the sweetness was still there.
He sat at his desk in his office in the university, I remember,
but when he rose to greet me his step was slow and the
upright carriage of his lean frame was halting. We talked, I
remember, and though it was with the usual easy interchange,
his thoughts came with a sort of weariness. The magnificent
brilliance flashed fitfully now and then instead of outpouring.
I did not stay long and I never saw him again. He remains,
nevertheless, a commanding figure in my life. In his person he
dramatizes for me the essential question of our modern age. Is
the creator to be held morally responsible for that which he
creates? Arthur Compton, physicist, was the son of a Christian minister. His mother was a Mennonite and a pacifist. He
was reared in the principles of human justice and peace—
especially of peace. Yet upon this great and kindly man was
placed the chief responsibility for the decision to develop the
first atomic bomb and finally to drop it. He tells his own story
in his book *Atomic Quest*, and from it I select these lines.
They contain the quintessence of his agony:

"The meeting at which Truman told Stalin of our intention
to use the new bomb was on 24 July. It was the previous
day that Colonel Nicols came to me at Oak Ridge with the
word. 'Washington wants at once the results of the opinion
polls on the use of the bomb.' I knew of the conference at

Potsdam, but of course knew nothing of the State Department and its discussions. The votes and petitions were now in my hands. I accordingly wrote out a message summarizing the results as objectively as I could and handed it to the Colonel. An hour later he came to me again. 'Washington wants to know what you think.'

"What a question to answer! Having been in the very midst of these discussions, it seemed to me that a firm negative stand on my part might still prevent an atomic attack on Japan. Thoughts of my pacifist Mennonite ancestors flashed through my mind. I knew all too well the destruction and human agony the bombs would cause. I knew the danger they held in the hands of some future tyrant. These facts I had been living with for four years. But I wanted the war to end. I wanted life to become normal again. I saw a chance for an enduring peace that would be demanded by the very destructiveness of these weapons. I hoped that by the use of the bombs many fine young men I knew might be released at once from the demands of war and thus be given a chance to live and not to die.

" 'My vote is with the majority. It seems to me that as the world stands the bomb should be used but no more drastically than needed to bring surrender.'

"Colonel Nicols took my message and sent it at once to Washington. Two weeks later the first bomb fell on Hiroshima."*

Yet I feel that he never completely convinced even himself. Else why did he repeat to me so often the record of his own struggle? Logically, mathematically, he believed the decision

* Reprinted by permission from the Oxford University Press from the book *Atomic Quest* by Arthur Holly Compton.

to drop the bomb was right. He believed that many lives were saved thereby and the cruel war brought to an end. Our military policy makers had decided to invade Japan in November. Conservative estimates were that in the inevitable hand-to-hand fighting of invasion, half a million Americans and two and a half million Japanese would be killed. Was it not better to bomb a city and force a surrender? This was the question Arthur Compton was forced to answer. I have put the story, through other characters, in my novel, *Command the Morning.*

His spirit lingered in the city, nevertheless. I thought of him often as we wandered the streets of St. Louis, and his memory did not leave me until the city prevailed. Prevail it did, through sheer magnificence and beauty. For St. Louis is magnificent with a grandeur that belongs to an opulent and almost Victorian past. The glitter of steel and glass has not taken over. Parks are vast, and in the St. Louis park there stands a conservatory fabulous in size, whole trees growing within the glass enclosure, surrounded by landscape tropical in colors of fruit and flower. The opera house, the theaters, are plush and elegant, and the people who walk the fine streets carry themselves in confidence. I confess that St. Louis is now ensconced within the small circle of my favorite world cities.

As for the convent—true, I know nothing of nuns and convents, but let this ignorance be balanced by my intimate knowledge of temples and monasteries in Asia. It began with the huge Buddhist temple that stood near my childhood home outside a Chinese city. I visited it often, and remember well the great images of the gods, especially the two mighty ones who stood in the entrance to the temple. I see myself a small

American girl in a summer frock of white Chinese linen—or perhaps it was blue—and I feel again the tremor of fear in my heart. The gods were so huge, one white, one black, their eyes rolled red and wild and in their hands they held forked spears. I always hastened past them to find the golden Goddess of Mercy, far in the last dim hall of the temple.

Something about the little American nun whom we met that day in the convent in Alton, Illinois, made me think of the goddess. She was not so beautiful, of course—for what woman can compete in beauty with the goddess?—but the look in the eyes was the same, benign, compassionate and distant from the world of men.

TFH: Dayton, Ohio, and another successful ball! You have told me that when writing of a situation or event out of one's life or imagination, one must find a hook, the thing most readily remembered, and build the story on that. I remember most about Dayton the look on that officer's face when you asked:

"Are there things you cannot explain?"

He was an officer from the UFO investigation installation in Dayton. We had learned of its existence too late to arrange for a visit so when this officer showed up at the ball I watched the old familiar thirst creep into your face as your need to know increased. When you asked your question, which you did at the earliest possible moment, he pulled on his ear lobe, turned very red, wet his lips, looked away and fidgeted in general. At last he looked at you and said—

PSB: Dayton, Ohio—yes, the ball was fun, but I had very much wanted to visit the installation for "the unidentifiable foreign objects"—in other words, such objects as flying saucers, et cetera. My insatiable curiosity, as you put it, does indeed compel me to ask the most inopportune questions at the most inopportune times, in the most inopportune places. But if I wait, they may never be asked. This time it had been too late to arrange for a visit to the installation and, besides, it was a Saturday. I could only plan for a visit some other time. It was at the ball, however, that I had a chance to ask the question I had wanted answered at the installation. I was introduced to the colonel. He came from the installation! Instantly I forgot the ball, the crowded room, the lights, the colors, the music. So far as I was concerned I was alone with the officer. We were at the head table, you remember, he with his wife, I beckoned to him while the band played a rumba. He came to my side and stooped to hear me.

"I am sorry we couldn't arrange a visit for you," he began. "Next time give me a little warning—"

I broke in. "I have one question."

"Yes?"

"Tell me if you can—are all the foreign objects that appear in the skies—or upon our earth—identifiable?"

He hesitated. Then he spoke.

"There are some we cannot identify."

My question was answered.

"Thank you," I said. "That is all I wanted to know."

He went back to his seat. You asked me to dance and we joined the crowd. But throughout the music and while we danced, my mind was wandering in the skies.

TFH: Back to Philadelphia for two weeks in the office broken only by short hops to Pittsburgh and New York for a ball in each city! There were still workmen all over the house, in and out of every crevice and corner, this time even on the roof installing central air conditioning. I marveled at our staff being able to accomplish anything as the utter confusion reached new peaks with each passing hour. Things were beginning to shape up, however, and we all looked forward to the day we would see workmen no more. I must say I've longed many times for the seeming peace and quiet of your trilogy, the *House of Earth*. Meantime, I am reminded of your rambling old farmhouse in which you now live and I know it's not all original. Tell me, did you have to put up with all of this mass confusion when your house was being rebuilt?

PSB: Oh, this house of mine! The curse of a too creative mind is that it never lets well enough alone. When I first saw my house—and it was before I was married and so it was my own house, bought with my money—I thought it would be big enough forever, my first house, in which I would live alone with my little adopted daughter. I was quite determined at that time never to marry again. The house was a hundred years old, a big living room with an ell for dining, and an old-fashioned kitchen. There were three bedrooms upstairs, a bath to be put in, upstairs again a huge attic, downstairs a huge cellar. The house was—and is—of field stone. It stands on a hill, it owns a big barn, a brook, a wood, four ponds, one very large, one very small, and two between.

TFH: Big enough? Then how did it grow to its present size? Eighteen rooms, six bathrooms, a swimming pool, tennis court, baseball field, the barn transformed into a play place for the whole community?

PSB: Well, the house grew with our life. I did marry again and the three of us began a new life there, for me my first real experience of my own country, my own people, my own house, for my little daughter her first adjustment to an

American home, for my husband, her adopted father, for him—what, I wonder? I doubt I am an easy woman for a man to live with—or perhaps I am too easy, too prone to yield in any argument, too ready to eat what is set before me, but slipping away too quickly into my secret life, that dwelling place of mind and spirit which only an artist knows, a solitary place, a refuge, a temple. Such a woman cannot be wholly possessed. Indifferent? No, not the word! I am never indifferent. I merely leave the door open between the outer life and the inner, and I enjoy both.

It was surprising to see how the house grew, it seemed almost of itself. We were always thinking of something new, more rooms for books, a window here, an alcove there. Outside we conceived terraces and pools, a boxwood walk to the pond, a locust walk to the gate, the dam in the brook to make a small lake, stalls in the lower barn for the children's ponies and their English cart, the long flower beds against the border of pines. We planted trees by the tens of thousands. The place grew and changed, shaped by our needs and imaginations, until suddenly it was finished forever.

For he died one day in early summer, before the little private porch outside his room was finished. He had been an invalid for a long time, not able to go downstairs, and I planned the upstairs porch, so that he could be carried out into the sunshine to see the big willows waving in the wind. We had planted them as twigs, no thicker than one's finger, and now they were great trees. That was how the years passed. After he died the house grew no more.

TFH: It was during this stopover at home that we decided to locate all of your manuscripts and move them into the Foundation. Few things have ever left me struck with awe to the extent of that half ton of paper! Jimmy and I had come out to your house one Sunday afternoon to help find the manuscripts and move them before leaving for our Western tour. It was a bright sunny day in mid-March, one of those days that fills you with the expectation of spring. We got out of the car and walked up the path to your door and I wondered what we would find. You were waiting, and we walked straight through your two libraries and the covered archway to the rear of the house and your office. I knew this chore of the manuscripts had to be done so I won a battle with myself, successfully overcoming the temptation to suggest a drive on such a beautiful day although I knew that you would welcome the idea, for we always aid and abet each other when it comes to clever little ways of avoiding a task. We sat side by side on the window seat in your office, the two of us, and cheered Jimmy on as he mounted the stepladder by the chimney piece and crawled into the cubbyhole closet above the fireplace. He opened the files there and began to hand down plain manila envelopes marked in longhand. *My Several Worlds* was first. The stack grew steadily. Paper! Yellow paper, white paper, notebook paper, typewriter paper. Originals, carbons, notebooks, galleys. Handwritten, typed, printed. Plays, novels, novelettes, stories, short and long. *The Exile, Fighting Angel, Sons, Dragon Seed, All Men Are Brothers, Imperial Woman*. From there we moved into the attic over your secretary's office. My God! A half ton of paper representing the life of a great author. *Command the Morning, Peony, Letter from Peking, The Mother, A House Divided*. All the while the comments from your corner were coming forth in a wee small voice.

"I'm sorry there is so much of this."

"Isn't this awful?"

"I can't imagine why I've written so much."

"That was a magazine serial."

"Those are plays. I've never done anything with them."

"No. *The Time Is Noon* has never been published. We felt it was too personal for that stage of my career. Perhaps I am ready to publish it now."

TFH: It must have taken courage for your publisher and you to stop *The Time Is Noon* even when it was already in galleys.

PSB: I remember, however, that he asked Dorothy Canfield, our old friend, to read the galleys before he made the final decision. She agreed with him. I accepted their decision without comment, although I knew the book had to be written for my own sake. I had to get rid of all my life until that moment—not my Chinese life, but my own private years. They had seemed endless when I was living them, an inadequate first marriage, a retarded child, a country I loved but that was not my own and now war-torn in a crisis of history. There was no hope ahead, so far as my eyes could see. And I was not sure whether I could enjoy the life in my own country or even adjust to it. After the years in an age-old culture, there were aspects of American life which seemed crude by comparison. I wondered whether I could live in so new a land, among a people so far from homogeneous. I confess now to hours, even days and weeks of doubt in those first years in my own country. In this mood I began to write *The Time Is Noon*.

Suddenly one day the air clarified and the fogs of doubt blew away. How and why I do not know. I had been writing out my thoughts and fears not in my own person, of course, but in a woman I had created out of myself. She too was beset. I had made her of the same substance as I myself was made, at that transitional moment. I was near the end of the book, I remember, but I did not know how to end it. There seemed to be no end. In the midst of this woman's insoluble problems she could come to no conclusion.

I remember the day, the morning, when the end came. I had risen early and going to my open window as I always do when I rise, to see how the world is and what the skies foretell, I beheld a fair scene. It was a day in early June. The roses were in bloom—my roses. The meadows were green—my meadows. And above them the sky was blue. Suddenly my life stretched before me, the years, the many years I had yet to live, good years, glorious years if I chose to make them so. I was still at high noon.

That, you will remember, is the way the book ends.

TFH: As the evening grew late, I remember, and we were still looking for, and finding, manuscripts in your attic that Sunday, I pulled out a play and began to read from it.

"I don't remember writing that," you said. You sat down on top of a packing crate and began to read aloud.

"This is rather good," you said in surprise. "We really should do something with this."

How I laughed at you! Now the manuscripts are safely locked up in the Foundation where they will stay. All but one! I still have the same old question and I must keep asking it until I receive a satisfactory answer. Where the devil is the manuscript of *The Good Earth?*

PSB: The devil has it! I simply cannot remember what I did with that manuscript. I remember writing the book in my attic room in the gray brick house in Nanking, China. My desk—the same one that now stands in the library of the Foundation house in Philadelphia—faced the window in that Chinese house. That wide window and the landscape beyond still live in my heart. I see the green lawn, the bamboos against the compound wall, the crowded roofs of the city beyond, then encircled by the great city wall. Beyond that wall rose Purple Mountain, its double crest clear against the sky or hidden in mist. I knew that mountain well, and know it, forever, its hidden temples, its tombs, the tombs of the Ming Emperors, its dells of ferns and sunny slopes blue with wild monkshead. At the desk I sat one spring, morning after morning for three months, writing my first real novel. As I have said, I had long wanted to speak for the voiceless peasants of China. Yes, quite true, I knew the intellectuals, too. They were articulate and self-satisfied. They could speak for themselves, but not for the peasants whom they did not know and indeed all but despised. I had learned to love those peasants, so brave, so industrious, so cheerful, expecting no help from others. Long ago I had made up my mind to be their voice.

In three months I told their story, typing the manuscript twice. What did I do with that manuscript? The copy I sent to my American publisher. The other? I doubt I even kept it. I did not know, I could not imagine, that a manuscript of mine could become valuable. Perhaps I threw it away as useless when the book was printed. Inexplicably the publisher's copy has also disappeared.

TFH: I remember that Sunday so well as we leave Reno bright and early on this April Easter. By the time the three of us had completed our search and loaded all the manuscripts into my car, it had grown late. It was eleven o'clock before we began unloading the car in front of the Foundation building on Delancey Place. It was quite a job, I must tell you. It had begun to drizzle rain about 9 P.M. and each stack of papers had to be covered with an old raincoat in order to transport them from the car to the house. Then into the elevator, load after load, and up to the fourth floor to be stacked in my room until a better place could be found. A pile of papers, more than two feet high, covering half the floor space in my large old bedroom! I sat on the foot of my bed until the wee, wee hours of the morning, stunned by the sight before me. They are all locked in a closet now waiting for a special fireproof vault being prepared for them. One day, in the distant future, those stacks of paper, some to be sold, some to be displayed, will supply the wherewithal to integrate thousands of displaced Amerasian children. I hope it pleases you to know the fate of your handiwork.

PSB: I am glad the manuscripts can be of use to such children. I had much rather have them so used than put behind glass doors in some university library. And there is no human group I'd rather have them used for than the Amerasian children, those who personify in their very being the two halves of my world. I confess my concern for them is partly because I am an American. For I saw Eurasian children in India, Indonesia and Indo-China in the days of empire and while I was sorry for their isolation, I felt no compelling necessity to do more than give them individual friendship. But these children, the Amerasians, are part of myself, my country, and I feel a moral responsibility as an American to be concerned at least to cooperate with those peoples among whom they have been born. Don't forget that in Asia a child belongs to his father, not his mother, and in this case the father is one of us, a boy born an American citizen, a youth educated in our homes, our schools, our churches, our communities, a young man in our armed forces, fighting or standing guard to maintain our faith in freedom for ourselves and all peoples.

Yes, I give my manuscripts gladly to these children who themselves prove the unity of the human race.

TFH: I lift my eyes from this page I am writing and I see the high crests of the Rocky Mountains. They are white with snow and glittering in the upper sunshine. But clouds hang over the lower slopes and the shadows are black.

> *Oh, beautiful for spacious skies*
> *For amber waves of grain.*
> *For purple mountain majesties*
> *Above thy fruited plains.*
> *America. . . .*

The words drift through my mind and I hum the tune to myself as we glide along a highway, wide and straight, with the Nevada hills green and purple and bare on the horizon. Ours is surely the most beautiful land in the world. This tour has been crowded with awe-inspiring sights. A scant three weeks ago we left Philadelphia by plane for Tucson, Arizona, on the first leg of our journey, and I think the part of me that has grown most weary on this trip is my eyes. "Look at this," "Look at that," has become the usual conversation. The Arizona desert, the California mountains, seashore and red-woods, quaint village after village nestled between magnificent cities—it all forms a living panorama of American life more moving and varied than I had remembered. I have seen all of this before, of course, in my many travels. This time it is different. Now I share your experience and joy in seeing it for the first time. I swell with pride, I confess, each time you say, "Never, anywhere in the world, have I seen anything to compare with this."

Our plane touched down in Tucson and we stepped out into the brilliant sunshine. The reception committee was impressive, I must say. The mayor, president of the Chamber of Commerce, our committee members and their friends, photographers and members of the press, and an Amerasian child and her adoptive family, she to present you with flowers, her mother to beam with pride. And proud she well should be of lustrous long black lashes framing beautiful eyes with a slight slant, dark brown hair, shining and curly, next to cream-colored skin on a face literally alive with a sparkle all its own. The little girl was new here, we found. Her mother told us of her arrival from Korea only a few months before and of her rapid adjustment to her new surroundings. It is a story we have often heard. This was a beautiful child, bright and charming. It is little wonder the Amerasians fast become the favorites of all who know them.

PSB: Do you think we should explain "hooks"? The term is mine—remember? We were talking about writing and the danger of slipping into a narrative that might become colorless and even dull and I said that one must recall the high moments in narrative experience and use those as points of emphasis, or "hooks," upon which to hang description, action, or emotion. Thus, while you describe so well the lovely Amerasian child, my own particular "hook," the instant of sharpest memory, is when, after she had presented me with the bouquet at the airport, the photographer asked her to repeat the performance so that he could get a picture.

"Go with the lady," the mother urged, wanting to be helpful. The child refused, you remember, and I saw panic on her little face. She ran to her mother and clung to her.

I knew exactly what the little girl was thinking. She remembered coming to that very airport, she remembered being met by a strange woman, she remembered her escort leaving her, never to return, and she feared being separated again this time from the person now her adoptive mother. How often I have seen this panic in children who have been moved from one place to another, one person to another, until they lose all sense of their own identity!

"Let her stay with you," I said to the mother.

TFH: The next day passed quickly filled with the usual press conference and rounds of television and radio interviews. The evening ended with a cocktail party in a charming home and dinner in a Chinese restaurant on the outskirts of town. We retired early with much excitement about the tour that awaited us the next day. We had been told about the underground missile bases circling Tucson and had asked to see one. A visit had been arranged. The Air Force officer and his aide greeted us early and led us out of town and through the desert and finally came to a stop before an innocent-looking mound of earth. I shall let you tell of the visit, my dear, except for the pride expressed by the officer and shared by all our group when you autographed their kitchen wall in indelible green ink. No President or Vice-President was ever asked to sign their wall we were told, but you, their favorite storyteller, were asked.

PSB: How shall I describe that missile? It is the greatest concentration of physical force that man has ever devised. We descended deep into the earth, three stories down, and there were five stories below into which we did not go. Here, far under the desert, men guard the monster we call the missile. We did not immediately enter into its presence. First we were shown the living quarters where the men eat, sleep and work. The kitchen was a pleasant place, eternally without the light of day, but brightly lit with man-made sunshine. The walls were smooth and white, and yes, I did take a pen as wide as a brush and put my name there boldly. Then we had coffee and pineapple upside-down cake, a homelike touch in that fearsome place. For I was conscious all the time of the monster, waiting in its den. We paused on our way to it, I remember, remarking on the youth of the men, especially of one who seemed to be in a responsible position, one demand-ing the utmost accuracy in a place where the slightest mistake might release the monster from its fetters.

"He is twenty-three," our guiding officer replied, "and wholly trustworthy."

It was good to know that there are young men like these serving in responsible positions. So, after cake and coffee and absorbing information, we proceeded through great heavy gates, each calculated to withstand the shock of explosion, until we found ourselves in the Presence. I have not often felt such awe. There the missile stood, poised and ready, quiver-ing, it seemed to me, with pent-up energy. We stood near its bluntly pointed top—near enough, that is, to see it but still far away, so vast the creature was. Through the latticed floor, we could look still farther down, far, far down to its base. I had a moment of pure terror. I wanted to run, to escape, to forget what was before my eyes, but I could not move. The officer was talking, he was telling us what the monster could do, its speed, its unerring accuracy, its totally devastating force. I thought I knew the fearful times in which we live, but I had not known the full and deadly potential.

"And what of you?" I asked the officer, "what of you if—"

"This place is built for survival," he said quietly, "and we shall survive."

And, strangely enough, in the midst of this terrifying place, another young man came forward to introduce himself and inquire if I had once an uncle who lived in Marshall, Missouri, which was his own home town. His mother had told him I had such an uncle, a Presbyterian minister.

A minister? I had six such uncles, all Presbyterian ministers except the rebellious one who defied the family by becoming Methodist. But Marshall, Missouri? Yes, I remembered, not because of the uncle, but because after what seemed to me too long a sermon one Sunday, we returned to the manse for a big family dinner, which is of no importance except for the dessert, which was ice cream. It was my first sight and taste of ice cream, an American delight of which I had heard but had never seen or tasted. It was fresh peach, I remember, home-made with pure cream, and I ate my way through a vast mound of it, I a child of naturally small appetite, reared as I had been in semitropical Asia! My mother watched me in consternation.

"Do be careful," she begged.

I came up bravely for more, I remember, and suffered no ill effects. And that was my introduction to ice cream and that was my memory of Marshall, Missouri. I shared it with the men in the missile base and for a laughing moment we forgot we were there.

TFH: The Tucson ball successfully behind us, we

headed west early on the morning after. My excitement mounted as we sped through the desert. Always ahead on the horizon were the foothills of the bleak stone mountains I knew we must cross before reaching the shore of the great Pacific. We stopped for luncheon in Calixico and tipped briefly below the border into Mexico. How dreadful the standard of living in a border town! It gives one what I am sure is an untrue picture of the country as a whole.

PSB: I have a theory that it is people who make the slums, not the slums the people. Take my own experience! I have five men on my farm in Pennsylvania. As you know, my place is several farms combined, each with its own stone farmhouse. Each house is modernized and comfortable. I take pride in providing good homes for the people who work on the farm. Now I am frankly discouraged. These good houses, clean and attractive when the farm families enter, quickly become slum-like. Too often the women are careless housekeepers, disorderly and lazy, and the men deserve nothing better. It is this, I think, which has made me decide to give up the farm and content myself with my own house. There is nothing so revealing of a person or a people as disorder. Slums? People create their habitation in their own image.

Anyone, however poor, can be clean, can be orderly, if he—or she—has the will for it—and the innate decency!

TFH: Rocks, stones, boulders, peaks, jagged rocks, smooth rocks, multicolored markers of past ages—try though we might we simply could not understand what holds those first California mountains together. They seemed to be just piles of loose rocks ranging in size from a hen's egg to a boxcar. We could not figure where the rocks had come from and what had created such a region. I watched you fret because you did not know. Not knowing is torture for you and you suffered because there was no one to ask. You commented on the lack of vegetation and kept a running barrage of "why do you suppose" until finally we came to a viewpoint with a snack shop and stopped. The wind tore at our clothes as we left the car on this the highest point of the mountain. In the shop was a man who tried in his innocence to answer your questions, himself puzzled as to why you wanted to know so much. At last he gave you some half-baked story about a prehistoric volcanic eruption that seemed to satisfy you for a time but I knew you would look up the area as soon as you possibly could in order to learn more.

PSB: I think he was right, vague though he was. This was not glacier country, and only some violent force could have thrown up those enormous boulders. The force pent up inside the earth is still the greatest natural force we know, and when it escapes through a fault in the precarious crust upon which we live it can cast up rocks as huge as ships and houses in its eruption.

TFH: We returned to the car and proceeded over the crest and down into fertile green valleys, literally dripping with the freshness of spring. And I do mean dripping, for it was the rainy season. Rain it did! Every single day of our California tour it poured, but even the nasty weather could not dim the beauty of that state. We skirted the edge of San Diego and swept up the coastal highway to Laguna for our first night in the state. They made special arrangements for us to have secluded accommodations, perched on the side of a cliff. We walked down a curving flagstone walk through brilliant gardens in full bloom to our sun deck, which hung out over the beach as though suspended from above. Your door opened to one side and mine to the other so it was like a private house. We went to bed immediately, for we were weary and had a full day of sight-seeing planned ahead. When I awoke the next day, with the sound of the sea so near, I could scarcely remember where I was at first. The day graced us with sunshine and the early rays came through my window brilliant and warm. I looked out and with a start found you already seated on the sun deck. I hurriedly dressed and joined you for coffee. We discussed the view before us and our excitement mounted for the day we had planned, San Juan Capistrano and south to La Jolla for luncheon, then back up the coast slowly, drinking in the beauty of our surroundings.

PSB: My two worlds of East and West often unite before my eyes. The bare mountains of California are like those that shaped the horizon of my childhood house in China. I love the wooded mountains of Vermont, but when I travel westward I am reminded of the mountains of Asia. Yes, and of the coves and inlets of sea and islands, and as if this were not enough, then in a shop in La Jolla we found the beautiful carved Kwanyin Goddess. We could not resist her gentle grace and we bought her, and had her shipped to Philadelphia. Now she stands in the wide hall outside the library looking as though she had been born there.

And you remember the fine collection of jade in that shop? Some rare pieces cost twenty or thirty thousand dollars. They were treasures from the palaces of Peking. Gradually these treasures are being sold secretly throughout the world, and most of them are now in museums and private collections in the United States. There is, of course, a considerable treasure on the island of Taiwan, transported thither by the Nationalist Chinese. I am glad for every beautiful piece that is safely in permanent museums in our country. There at least it is protected.

And speaking of jade, I had not known until we stopped at the shop in a hotel in Salt Lake City that our own Wyoming produces some quite good jade. There was a display of it in that shop—remember? Thus jade, my favorite stone, is not only Asian, as I had thought, but also American.

We had a sentimental pleasure in seeing Capistrano, where the swallows return every year. I don't wonder that anyone returns to that charming place, where history pervades. I am glad there has been no effort to restore the ancient Spanish buildings. Let them remain as time has left them!

Los Angeles? Well, I had been there before. This time I will remember only the few people I want to remember. Let me think of the pleasant Sunday morning spent in Steve Allen's home, with his wife Jane Meadows. She, too, and her sister Audrey, are Americans who, like me, had their first years in China. And Shirley MacLaine joined us from her home nearby, and she, with home and husband and child in Japan, belongs to East and West.

As if this were not mixture enough, we were joined by my Chinese friend Lily and her husband, a brilliant young scientist, and their small son, Little Pear. It is of this child that I have written in my book, *The Living Reed*, in the incident when Yul Chun returns to his family house by night and meets for the first time the son of his brother. The recognition there between man and child is a true picture of the first time that Little Pear and I met. His family was living in Philadelphia and they came to visit me one Sunday afternoon. Little Pear was then ten months old. It was the first time I had seen him. He was a large handsome child, well mannered and calm. He sat quietly on the sofa with his parents, and I made no effort at further acquaintance, for I have learned from long experience that it is the child who should make the next approach after casual greetings. He sat gazing at me thoughtfully, and suddenly I was impelled to speak to him.

"Little Pear, are you ready to come to me?" I asked.

He came instantly. He climbed on my lap. He embraced me, he leaned back to look at me intently, he laughed with joy and embraced me again and again, breaking into fresh laughter. I was astounded, for though I am happy that children like me, I had never had such recognition as this. His parents were as astonished as I was.

"Never," his mother declared, "never have we seen him like this, not even with us! He seems to recognize you. It is as though he had seen you before in another life."

It was like that. I cannot explain it but it was like that. And each time we meet now it is as though we had not parted. There is a renewed recognition. That day in Steve Allen's house, Lily and her husband took us to luncheon at a Chinese restaurant, you remember. They had their own car but as a matter of course Little Pear climbed into our car and sat quietly at my side the whole way.

Do I believe in the pre-existence of the individual soul? If I believe, it is because I cannot otherwise explain the fact that one is powerfully attracted to certain individuals and not to others, and this attraction is far more than physical. We shall see, we shall see, and some day we shall know as we are known.

And no, in reply to your question, I shan't say anything more about the people of California. Well, yes, I'll make an exception and he is the Chinese owner of that beautiful shop in Chinatown, San Francisco, a city in itself an enchantment, although its steep hills are somewhat alarming. There was a pair of Kwanyins there in that shop with whom you fell in love, I could see, and on our last day you could not resist going back for a last look at them.

I did not join you in this rendezvous but remained in the car. Suddenly you called me, saying that I must come in, that you had found a treasure. I obeyed, and the owner, bowing politely and pleased to recognize me, showed me an exquisite piece of jade carved into the image of Woo Sung, the hero of the great and ancient Chinese novel, *Shui Hu Chuan*, which I have translated under the title of *All Men Are Brothers*. In this piece there were four different colors of jade, a most rare sight. Under the figure the shop owner had placed a legend: "Woo Sung, hero of the novel, *All Men Are Brothers*, translated by Pearl S. Buck."

I was touched, but I was careful not to praise it too much lest I seem to be suggesting a gift. But of course now we had to buy the pair of Kwanyins, I am happy to say, and we did. Then as we were about to leave, this courtly and highly cultivated Chinese gentleman presented me with a piece of white jade carved as a medallion. Him I will remember!

TFH: Whoa! Back up! There are others I am sure you will want to remember. Our teen-aged committee leader near San Francisco—remember? I called the office from the hotel the day we arrived to get her telephone number. The office only knew her name and address in Redwood City. As luck would have it the first one the operator called was right. I spoke with Becky, then with her mother. The next day they came to the Fairmont to see us with some of her friends who are also working for the Foundation. We heard how these teen-agers made candles for Christmas and sold them for the Amerasian children. We heard of the ladies' head scarfs they are making and selling now. It was heartwarming indeed to see the youth of one country working for the youth of another. Give us a hundred Beckys!

PSB: Very well, I will remember Becky and her friends and mother and with pleasure, for they were delightful people. For the rest, California remains for me a place of superb natural beauty, sea and coast, forests and mountains, a land of which we can all be proud, at least for natural beauty. But I remember too many beauties to enumerate. Let me speak only of the redwoods I had always longed to see and which far surpassed what I had imagined. I stood in their mighty presence, and felt past ages encompass me. Their roots were in primeval earth, and their tops seemed to touch the sky. Let all Americans be grateful to those patriots who, loving our country truly, prevented the destruction of these great trees. Yes, there were others who would have cut them down to common wood and sold them for private gain. How can the ones who prevented this crime be sufficiently rewarded? At least they should receive our highest honors.

And with this conclusion, I leave California.

TFH: There were balls in Fresno and Sacramento, and then on to Reno. What a strange little city, nestled in quiet hills! People gambling furiously, their faces intent, their eyes seeing only that which they are doing. And the hotel owners are clever! If one wishes to register one must walk first by the slot machines. There is no television or radio in the rooms. There is absolutely nothing to do in the entire town except gamble or leave it and sight-see in the country around it. Even to enter the dining room or coffee shop one must pass the twenty-one tables. To go to the bar one must pass roulette. To go to the rest room one must weave among the dice tables. And they say the marriage and divorce mill is equally as big a business. We stayed in the same hotel in which you stayed during the visit you told of in *My Several Worlds*.

PSB: The same hotel but this time with memories of twenty-five years of happy marriage, so all the sadness of the first visit is forgotten. For it is sad that any marriage should end in divorce. Much goes into the making of a marriage and in divorce all that is lost. Remember the middle-aged woman who sat by the window in the hotel dining room and watched her little dog chained outside? I could tell by her face that she was getting a divorce and that the dog was all she had now. She recognized me and came to our table to talk about my books, to ask for an autograph, to leave a gift for the Amerasian children. Suddenly her heart was too full and she had to tell us of her circumstances, and grief overflowed in her last words.

"It didn't have to be," she kept saying. "It just didn't have to be. Maybe ours wasn't a really happy home, but it could have been normal, just normal."

Her eyes turned to the patient little dog, and she went on:

"My daughter wants the dog, but I said I had to have something. So I'm keeping the dog, I told her. Until death do us part—"

Yes, divorce is heartbreaking, however it takes place. Enough of it!

Reno? The contrast between that garish cheapness and the magnificence of the surrounding landscape—that is what I remember. If I were a tourist I'd travel ten thousand miles to see Pyramid Lake and Lake Tahoe and Virginia City and— wait, here's something odd. In one of the old hotels in Virginia City the proprietress was a woman no longer young but very cheerful and busy. She hailed me with a Chinese greeting and the announcement that she had lived in Peking, had been to many parts of China and was indeed a veteran traveler in Asia. Again the strange meeting of East and West took place, this time high in the spectacular mountains of Nevada.

TFH: We drove from Reno on to Salt Lake City before dinner, having made it habit to rise early before any leg of our journey. Our next ball, if you will remember, was in Davenport and the one after that in Omaha. As it is necessary to go through Omaha to get to Davenport from the Great Salt Lake, we made elaborate plans as to how we were going to sneak through Omaha to avoid publicity. Ha! It was like trying to sneak through a smoker with Gypsy Rose Lee. We were, of course, recognized at every turn and had to promise all kinds of personal interviews on our second stop, if people would only keep our first visit quiet. Everyone agreed and on we went to Davenport for three full days. My assistant, who travels with us much of the time now, had everything so well in hand that it gave us more free time than usual. We were in the middle of a flood and that mighty river there had overrun its banks and swept all in its path downstream. We could see it from our windows, just a block away, and out beyond the water's edge we could see the tops of trees and roofs. We were told the waters would crest in two days and vowed we would walk close enough at least to say we had been in the flood. That walk was our downfall. We passed a small jewelry shop and there in the window we saw a three-piece French clock set in the exact same marble of the fireplace of our dining room. It was over a hundred years old and of a dainty classic design. It worked perfectly. It was reasonable. It now sits on our dining room mantel. With just one block more to walk we found the ancient Italian marble statue fated to sit in a planter in front of our building. Two children carved beautifully in white marble hold up a large oyster shell in which we will plant some evergreen. In that block we found the saltcellars of hand-wrought silver that grace our dining table and the white cocks you spoke of earlier, under Chen Chi's *Good Earth*. We were about to visit a few more shops when our traveling companions threatened to lock us in the hotel room, paint the windows black, and throw the key away. We have an impatience to finish anything, the two of us, and most other people simply do not understand this drive.

PSB: Yes, delays drive us unanimously frantic. I never thought I'd find my equal in this respect, but there are times when you even surpass me.

As for the flood, you must remember that I spent more than half the years of my life on the banks of the mighty Yangtse. I know that our Mississippi is a big river, but in comparison to the Yangtse it is only a big brook. Still, I had never seen our river in flood, and my memories of flood are Chinese. The last time I saw the Yangtse in flood the city of Nanking, seven miles away, was under water. The river flooded far beyond the city walls into the countryside, isolating villages and ruining fields until the waves splashed at the foot of Purple Mountain.

Therefore when we heard that Davenport was threatened by flood, I saw us marooned there perhaps for weeks. I was less alarmed when I saw the reality. It was not a pleasant sight, nevertheless. The muddy water was creeping up the street in front of the hotel until it was in the next block. How many times I rose from my bed in the night to see by the light of the moon how much nearer the water was!

We stayed for the ball in spite of it and left at midnight to drive to Omaha, reaching there at dawn. Two hours of sleep and we began another day.

TFH: Omaha stands out in my memory for two reasons. The ball was well planned and well carried out, but equally as important, I was made an honorary citizen. It was my first such honor and that city will always be a special place for me. On these trips I've come to understand so well President Kennedy's wonderful remark, "I'm the man who came to Paris with Jackie."

Chicago offered our most successful affair sponsored, not by a dance studio, but a group of ambitious young businessmen. The hook there? I can only remember that we attended eighteen press meetings, one luncheon and two dinners in two short days before our flight back to Philadelphia. We knew then that this was our last real tour. We plan to have many benefit affairs, yes, but no more "whistle-stops." We have accomplished our purpose—many people everywhere have taken these children to their hearts, and there they will remain.

As I read over this manuscript and make final corrections, I know that it is not finished. It cannot end here. I sit in the solarium of our Foundation house on Delancey Place. The early morning sun comes through the glass roof and warms all that is here with its energy. Our green parrot cavorts like a circus clown on his favorite perch. Of all those places in the house where he sits, he has found one he likes best. It is a six-inch prong of wrought iron that once held up its half of a glass shelf on what was a baker's rack in some bygone era. Now this rack stands, its black made very black, its brass polished and gleaming, on one side of the archway that leads to the dining room. Instead of sweet-smelling, freshly baked goodies, its shelves hold our potted plants, collected from here and there, the palms from Florida and miniature fruit trees from California, and that new hedgelike bush with white flowers that we rushed out and bought the other afternoon to fill that empty space there. Another rack exactly like this one stands on the other side of the arch, but do you think our bird will sit on it? Never! If he is placed there he will climb down and walk to the other side and work his way up to the one where he now sits. He chats gaily to himself, "Hello, Polly," "Polly wants a cracker," "What'cha doing?" "Where is Hattie?" Then he giggles madly as Hattie, our treasured housekeeper, and our green bird's favorite person, gets off the elevator with her cheery "Good morning." Now she makes coffee and the tempting aroma drifts out of the kitchen and she hums happily to herself and the bird hums right along and life begins in our house for another day.

Soon the office staff will come in downstairs and our work faces a new day with great zest. Three members of our staff have just returned from Korea, and they have brought back with them many experiences with the people and with our children. They tell of babies suffering malnutrition and of young children not being educated, sleeping in unheated huts, huddled together against the cold. They tell how unscrupulous people who head some of the orphanages steal food intended for the children and sell it. They tell how blankets and powdered milk sent by American agencies can be bought on the black market. Their reports have made us know that we cannot support any orphanage or school or day-care center unless we have our own Korean social worker stationed in that place to see to it that our aid indeed goes to the children as intended. And we have decided we must pay our Korean workers better than other agencies do, so that they will be more apt to do as we wish and less likely to steal. We know now also that our American representative in that or any country must be a man thoroughly schooled and experienced in business procedures, for ours is the business of integrating these new children into the societies in which they are born and must live. Meanwhile our work goes on. Already many American families are supporting or educating the children born in Asia, fathered by our American servicemen.

PSB: For some of them, alas, it is too late. They are already grown. Or is it too late? I have before me this morning a handful of typewritten pages. They came in the morning's mail from Korea. They tell the story of a young girl, the child of an American man and a Korean woman. This girl is now eighteen. She has brown hair, violet eyes, fair skin, a nose not Asian in its contour. Her mother is a Korean woman. This woman came to a Korean city fresh from the country when she was only eighteen herself. It was in the early days of the Liberation. She was working in a little shop as a clerk when an American soldier entered. He was impressed by her good looks, she was impressed by his charm, they became friends, and soon she was pregnant.

Was she therefore a prostitute? It did not occur to her that she was. They were married by Korean religious rites. What she did not know until he left her was that such a marriage can only be legal if it is registered in the American Consulate.

He had not registered it, nor did he tell her he was never coming back. Perhaps he thought he was. They had spent some happy months together. But when she knew at last that she was alone, to become a prostitute was her only way of making a living. Into this life her daughter was born.

The sight of the blue-eyed child made the Korean mother both sad and angry—sad, for she had loved the man, angry because the child looked like her father. With these mixed feelings she tried to be just to the child. She saw to it that the child went to school and had enough food. School was not easy. The other children teased the blue-eyed girl. They called her High Nose, and Half Blood. In her loneliness the girl sometimes ran away and hid in the mountains. Yet hunger always compelled her to come home again. Her mother never went to the school with her. She did not like to be seen with her daughter. Nevertheless she did go to the graduation exercises on the day the young girl got her diploma. And by then she had given up prostitution and was trying to make a living by selling vegetables.

It was too late for the girl, however. Her mother had been known as a prostitute, and so the girl was irrevocably the daughter of a prostitute. She could find no respectable employment. And new Americans were here, young fresh-faced men scarcely older than she, who was now in her mid-teens. The Americans had money, money, money, and she was starving.

Even then she might have resisted the handsome young man from Texas. But she was vulnerable. Never had she loved anyone, unless it had been her mother's old father. No, she had not loved her mother. Why? Because there was an incident she could not forget. Once, when she was very small, not more than four years old, she remembered that she and her mother and the old man were fleeing to escape a battle. She could not walk fast enough, and she began to cry. But her mother paid no heed, not even when she could walk no more and sank into the dust of the road.

"Take the child on your back," the old father told the mother.

"Leave her," the mother said. "Shall I lose my life for that foreign brat? We'll go on!"

The old man had sighed. "Is she not our offspring, too?" he said, and he lifted her to his own back.

Alas, he had not survived the cruel journey and so how could she love her mother? That woman had deserted her finally. One morning she had waked alone in the small hut which was their home. Her mother was gone and never seen again.

So, when the tall American offered the girl a chocolate bar that same winter's day, she accepted it, and then their acquaintance became friendship.

I can trust him, she thought.

She became his wife in fact, if not in law.

He rented a small house, and spoke of marriage. He told her that in his country it was usual for man and woman to live together before marriage. She believed him. She came into his house, and she waited impatiently for the final ceremony.

It never came. He was called home. A long kiss, his promise, his parting accusation—

"You don't trust me! I'm coming back, darling!"

But he has never come back. She was alone in the house. Not for long, however! He had left unpaid debts, the rent, the food. What could she do? She accepted another man—another, another.

Today she is eighteen. Ten times she has been pregnant. Ten times she has refused to bear a half-American child.

"It is the least I can do," she says.

She is only one of many, except that she is braver than most. Others are not destroying themselves in her fashion. Amerasian children give birth to other Amerasian children and these children plead for their fathers. I open now a letter from Okinawa.

"I am half-American," the scrawling script declares. "Can you please to find my American father. His name is ———. He lives at ———. This my mother tell me before dying last year. I am ask nothing—only once to see him or if not possible only one letter, to prove I am American like him."

We get these letters from the Six Countries we call *our* countries. They are Korea, Japan, Okinawa, Taiwan, the Philippines and Vietnam. In each the Amerasian children search for their place in the world. They speak for themselves and they speak through the young American who represents us now in Korea, our pilot country. I hear his voice recorded on a tape and flown across land and sea. He says:

"I have begun interviewing caseworkers and we start work on Monday. We are interviewing only fresh young people, who have a new approach to these new children. I shall ask them to bring in studies on six children a day. With six men workers this means thirty-six children a day will be found and reported on. In a few weeks we will have the first five hundred children.

"I am realizing that *education* is what the children need. As the Amerasian child grows older we run into problems. The mother takes care of her baby somehow, but as she grows older and older—well, take Miss Kim, for example. Certainly she cannot go back to being a party girl. She doesn't look like one any more and her child is eleven years old, a boy, and he is getting no education at all.

"As far as Company A's enlargement—I received your letter which states that you want room for another 100 children there. I assume that you sent this letter before you saw what the situation was with the last report which I mailed to you about the wooden barracks now being readied and probably to be done by this weekend. That whole shooting match, which was the winterizing of the wooden barracks, will give us room for 32 boys in that wooden barracks. Our servicemen are putting in two heaters, they have put in new walls, new ceiling, painting, and also we are putting in a hot-water heating system in the shower room, so that the children will have hot water instead of just cold water, with new pipes, new fixtures, and also making available at a future date to have the water piped up to the kitchen. This whole job—the barracks and the boiler room, I suppose we'll call it—was going to cost a total of $940. So we talked to Capt. Rathnow and Sgt. Martin and we finally came up with a deal that I wrote to you about, so that it will cost us $300 which I have already committed and all of that work will be done. The Army is going to pay the rest of it themselves so we will have $940 worth of work done but it is going to cost us $300 and we will make available an additional 32 beds which will give us room for 32 boys and 40 girls."

Records of the children are pouring in. Yes, we are finding them, hidden away in villages, swarming about army camps with their mothers, wandering in city streets, sleeping under bridges and in culverts. The records are sadly alike:

Father—unknown American
Mother—Korean prostitute
Country of birth—Korea

Sometimes there is a change.

Chan Yung—boy aged ten—father unknown American—mother Korean who died six years ago. Child taken by aging widow now destitute. Mother was talented in music and art. Pay special attention to this child. Very bright—never been to school.

And here is a little girl, unknown American father, lives with Korean mother and two Amerasian brothers, all different fathers, all unknown.

Kap-yung—aged three—father American unknown. Mother Korean unknown. Child abandoned at age of one month and sheltered by finder, herself a beggar.

Mi-yan—the mother escaped from Seoul in the Communist invasion during the Korean war and was raped by an American soldier. Her husband was among the missing and she has always been poor. Yet she has never lived in the areas of the American camps nor sought any association with the men. She manages somehow to support her son by a bare subsistence. He even went a few years to primary school.

Lee-sang—father American unknown—mother Korean. Child lives with mother in slums and she seldom finds work and is not a prostitute. Child seriously undernourished. Must be fed before he can go to school.

Taik-yin—father American unknown—mother Korean returned from prostitution now a day laborer—child hungry and no education.

Brothers and sisters—father American unknown—deserted by Korean mother—living on streets in Seoul, begging, as they have no family or relatives.

Soo-tak—father American—lives with Korean mother—received letters and money from father until age of 8, when everything stopped completely.

Soo-won—father American, legally married to Korean mother before his return to USA. Since then, father is missing or hiding.

Sung-yi—this child is the product of an outrage during the war by an American soldier. The mother has never been a prostitute. Her husband, having no child of his own, loves this boy and wants to educate him, since he is very intelligent. But the man is only a poor tenant farmer and there is little he can do.

Yung-sun—father American unknown, mother Korean. Child abandoned but found by a good but very poor Catholic family and raised as their daughter. One of the most beautiful Amerasian girls we have seen.

Ye-poon—father American unknown—mother Korean who married another GI and went to USA to live, abandoning child then six years old.

Leon—father American unknown—child has lived with mother since birth. She expects another Amerasian child next month by different father. Being pregnant, she has been idle for five months—extremely poor—needs help. She asks us to take her new baby for adoption, or anything, whether girl or boy.

Johnny—has lived with his grandmother since birth. His mother is in Seoul trying to find a job. She has given up prostitution. Actually she has never been in the business. When she was only 18 she met a GI and lived with him and bore his child. He went home and she does not want to be associated with GI's any more.

Dennie—is only a month old. His American father left Korea two days after his birth, leaving no address, no nothing. Child is weak and undernourished.

Jackie—since birth lived with mother and American father. Father returned to USA last year, since when no word has come.

Stephen—born 7 months after American father left Korea. He is still less than a month old. Mother unable to work, no source of income, child is in bad condition needing medical help.

The lists of the children roll on and on, into infinity. They are not the lists of the young dead, the names of the day's casualties on the strange battlefields of today's world, centered in obscure points of Asia, Africa, South America. No, these children are the lists of the living. Yet they, too, are casualties of war. Their fathers should have been other young men, gentle lads, tilling the fields of Vietnam, or fishing the indented seas of Korea and Okinawa. Or else let it be that their mothers should have been young American girls, vital with health and gaiety. But there has been war, there is war, and young American men have impregnated strange women in lands far from their own. Of this meeting a new people is being born. Shall this new people, innocent and helpless in childhood, bear the whole burden of our times? My heart, my mind, say no—no and never! The danger of children born without love, without hope, is too great. I dare not refuse the challenge. And I am not alone. I have chosen young men and women to help me, since I myself am no longer young. It is fitting that the young accept responsibility. For the problem of those new children is the problem of youth, and it is young men and women who must solve it.

TFH: You chose us because we are young, because we are dedicated. Our basic staff at the Foundation is younger even than I. Fresh out of school, a brilliant determined group, they are maturing through your guidance, so that our job will continue with the same concepts with which we began. Your concept, desires and dreams will be fulfilled as they are already being fulfilled. Our search teams are going into our Six Countries, we are combing the villages, the countryside, the cities, seeking everywhere the new child who has the eyes of old Asia and the strong body of new America. We find him ill, undernourished, neglected, despised, but struggling to live. We feed him, heal him, guide him and send him to school. Our goal is to help him to be a blessing to the land of his Asian mother, a pride to the land of his American father. An idea born in your heart, and of a need you saw, The Pearl S. Buck Foundation will continue to express the greatness for which you stand as long as I live, and forever, Amen!

We have covered our land on these tours, the North and South of it, the East and West of it, from sea to sea. Over and through mountains, deserts, orchards and plains, stopping in seventy-five cities, with more to come, we tell the American people everywhere about the new people, the Amerasians. You have inspired them with your energy and drive, taking to the road like a gypsy, at your stage of life, and for these children. And Americans are responding generously!

As for me, my heart swells with pride in our country. I feel a song in my being:

> *America—America!*
> *God shed his grace on thee,*
> *And crown thy good with*
> *Brotherhood* . . . .
> . . . . !
> SANS END